# MEADOW LAKE
# GOLD TOWN

# MEADOW LAKE

## GOLD TOWN

~~~~~~~~~~~~~~~~~~~~~~~~~~~~~~~~~~~~~~~~~~~~~~~~~~~~~~~~~~~~~~~

## by PAUL FATOUT

BLOOMINGTON

INDIANA UNIVERSITY PRESS

LONDON

For Roberta

# Contents

# Foreword

A few years ago I journeyed from Nevada City, California, to Marysville in a red-white-and-blue station wagon that was both United States mail car and bus for three or four of us who rode along. The trip was one of the most enjoyable I ever made anywhere. We rambled roundabout via peaceful back roads that meandered over Nevada and Yuba Counties, pine-forested brown foothills giving way to valley fields and the green crops of ranchers, our R. F. D. driver stopping frequently at roadside boxes and village postoffices to deliver and to pick up mail. In no hurry, we were content to travel at a leisurely pace through countryside somnolent under the languorous summer sun of interior California, while gold rush history unfolded before us.

Our starting point, familiar to early settlers as Deer Creek Dry Diggings, is a flourishing survivor in its second century, its graceful white balconies, gabled houses, and gingerbread woodwork possessing dignity and charm. In Nevada City the past seems close enough to evoke in imagination the heady climate of the 1850's, and to people the hilly streets with pioneer characters, like Eleanore Dumont, the decorous and smartly-dressed lady gambler known as Madame Moustache. She ran her own popular gaming saloon, where she dealt blackjack with considerable success.

On our route were shrunken remnants of Smartville and Timbuctoo, forlorn remains of places bustling with vitality over a hundred years ago. A few weathered buildings marked the site of the celebrated town of Rough and Ready, which for decades maintained its status as an independent state, and where legend says that Lotta Crabtree, the precocious child protégé of Lola Montez, delighted an audience of miners by singing and dancing, her stage a blacksmith's anvil.

The once-roaring camps have long been silent, but mining goes on in that region. At one of our stops, near the Yuba River, an offshore craft, blunt of bow and graceless as a floating packing box, was dredging up auriferous mud from the bed of the stream. Our driver, after making his collection at headquarters there, nonchalantly flung into the car a canvas bag heavy with ingots of gold. With superb indifference, he did not place this provocative bundle carefully on the front seat where he could keep an eye on it, but casually tossed it in among other parcels as off-handedly as if it were nothing more valuable than a piece of trivial junk mail.

I thought of the sturdy old Concord coaches of Wells Fargo's Express rattling over mountain trails, often with a cargo of raw gold and bullion in the treasure box under the driver's seat, driver and shotgun messenger alert to get the drop on bandits. These bold outlaws, if not deterred by persuasive gunfire, were likely to hold up the coach, seize the treasure, and relieve gentlemen passengers of money and watches with their heavy gold and silver chains, generally lifting the ladies' jewelry also, but once in awhile gallantly refraining.

I recalled the most famous, or notorious, highwayman of those parts: Black Bart, the mild-mannered thief, who held up twenty-eight stages single-handed, making his exploits galling to the authorities by leaving at the scene of the crime sardonic verses that mocked efforts of company detectives to catch him. For almost a decade he eluded them all, only to be apprehended at last by the evidence of a laundry mark on a handkerchief. Other road agents, too, were momentarily successful, and not a few bit the dust.

Our twentieth-century mailman, however, shrugged off the

hypothetical threat of banditry as scarcely worth serious attention. He carried no shotgun upright and ready to hand by the
driver's seat, no revolver in a holster on the hip, not even a
modest .22 strapped to the steering post. His unconcern with
possible thieves was vast and bored, but it was justified, for
we rolled placidly ahead without running into an ambush of
masked gunmen. The sackful of gold bullion and we few travelers—whose meager collective booty in money and other loot
would hardly have paid a robber for his time anyway—reached
Marysville without melodramatic incident.

The episode was a reminder that gold is still there in the
vicinity of the Mother Lode, still being sought, though nowadays
by methods more elaborate and costly than the elementary digging and panning of the prospector of '49. Perhaps, as the narrative of Meadow Lake may imply, and as the speculations of some
modern mining specialists suggest, gold also lies hidden in the
locale of this book, the granite mountains of the high Sierras. At
least, a great many fortune-hunters once believed it was there,
and went after it with dogged determination if with no brilliant
success.

The text that follows attempts to delineate the history of
their feverish search, spurred on by rosy expectations that
faded under the blight of disappointment: these varying states
of mind accompanying the rise and fall of a mining town founded
upon confidence in future prosperity, yet, like other California
camps, going down in the ruin of failure. The cycle of upsurge-
and-decline is familiar in that region, but the chronicle of the
Meadow Lake district is unusual because it spans almost a
century, a long time for a mining locality. Furthermore, the wide
gap between the extravagant expectations that created the
transitory "city" and the collapse of hopes that destroyed it
makes its fate spectacular.

The story is pathetic in that, whereas elsewhere in gold
country tottering buildings and crumbling walls testify to the
existence of communities that in flush times were alive and tur-

bulent, up at the summit no sign remains of human habitation. Nothing stands to tell the visitor that here thousands of people swarmed and labored, stubbornly pitted themselves against wilderness and hard Sierra winter, assailed the grim granite ridges, and built what they firmly believed would become a metropolis, long-lived and lusty. That so tremendous an outpouring of energy and so much faith in eventual triumph should have left no trace are painful commentaries on the vanity of human wishes. Of many California localities that have illustrated the flow and ebb of golden aspirations, Meadow Lake, though it has vanished from the face of the earth, is an eloquent example.

For assistance in assembling the materials of this book I am grateful to the helpful people of the Bancroft Library, University of California, Berkeley: John Barr Tompkins, Cecil Chase, Alma Compton, Irene Moran, Linda Schieber, Estelle Rebec, Janice Koyama, Vivian Fischer, Cort Smith, Roland Mayer, Fritz Lichty, Peter Lawrence, David Hopper, Pat Howard, William Cady, Marie Byrne. The Bancroft is a splendid place to work, not only because of its wealth of western resources, but also because of its amiable staff. A good source of information is the History Room of the Wells Fargo Bank, San Francisco, another agreeable workshop, thanks to its Director, Irene Simpson, and her assistants. My best thanks to Donna J. Payne, forbearing editor of the Indiana University Press; to Fred Anderson and aides, The Mark Twain Papers, University of California, Berkeley; to Don Baxter, Pacific Gas and Electric Company, San Francisco; to Miriam Pike and others, The California State Library, Sacramento; to Robert Paine, Nevada City, California; and to Ed W. Kiessling, State of California Division of Mines and Geology, San Francisco. My wife, Roberta, deserves an award of merit for once again bearing up under the storm and stress of book-making, no mean achievement as anybody knows who has ever been through it as either writer or observer. Doing a book is a demanding affair that is often hard on body and spirit, yet a task that is, to me, always absorbing and fascinating. Digging up material, writing, revising, proofing and so forth are, as Huck Finn said of the statements in *Pilgrim's Progress,* "interesting but tough." I am sure that Roberta would subscribe to at least half of that remark.

P. F.

# MEADOW LAKE
# GOLD TOWN

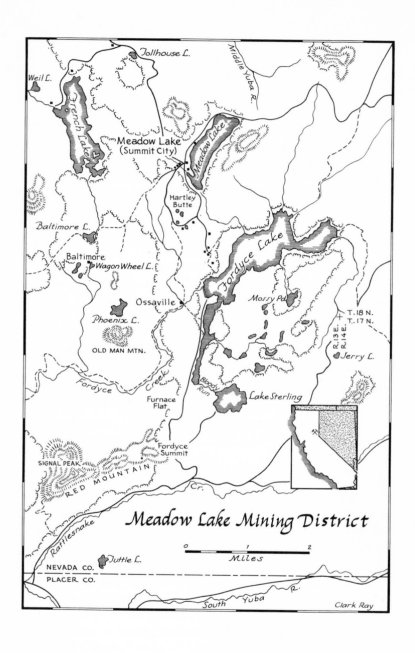

Meadow Lake Mining District

# 1

## The Big Thing

THE MEN of a gold rush mining camp were nomadic adventurers ready to move on the moment faroff hills beckoned with promise of greater rewards. Pausing in one locality, staking claims there and working leads, or perhaps only hanging around doing nothing much in particular, gold-seekers were easily enticed away by news of rich strikes in a remote gulch or a territory far over in the hazy blue of distant mountain ranges. One of "The Miner's Ten Commandments" (1853) admonished the miner: "Thou shalt not go prospecting before thy claim runs out." But when an El Dorado loomed many miles off yonder, that directive was more honored in the breach than in the observance.

Always elsewhere was the sought-for bonanza—the big thing—made luminous by the enchantment of distance. The constant search for it produced a human flow as restless as the tides and as compulsive. One camp named Git-up-and-Git spelled out an imperative for all camps. All were of like mind with the man of Coloma, weekday miner and Sunday preacher, who announced to his ragged congregation before the benediction: "There will be divine service in this house next Sabbath—if, in the meantime, I hear of no new diggin's!"

Up and down the Mother Lode of California and adjacent

country, a region several hundred miles long and about fifty miles wide, ranged the forty-eighters, the forty-niners and later arrivals, marking their passage by such earthy place names as Red Dog, Fiddletown, You Bet, Humbug, Squabbletown, Gouge Eye, You-be-Damned, Bedbug, Shirt-Tail Cañon, Pinch-em-Tight, Mad Mule Gulch, Growlersburg, Bootjack. Sometimes they added "City," either as a gesture of derision for an uncitified layout or as a token of future grandeur expected to descend upon an unsightly conglomeration of tents and shacks: Henpeck City, Potluck City, Brandy City, Hell-Out-for-Noon City. These places did not become metropolitan. Neither did New Chicago or New Philadelphia.

Before long big things attracted. Gold excitement at Fraser River caused a rush of more than 20,000 to British Columbia. Walker's River got them, the Cariboo Mountains, Kern River, Pike's Peak. In the early 1860's the supposedly inexhaustible silver of the Comstock Lode in Nevada Territory sent great swarms of treasure-hunters surging over mountain passes into Washoe. They remained long enough to build Virginia City before setting out for Esmeralda, Reese River, Salmon River, Santa Rita Mountains, Excelsior, White Pine, and that other Virginia City in Idaho—some returning to the Comstock during the Big Bonanza of the 1870's.

Stampeding to the Black Hills of Dakota in 1876–80 were gray-haired veterans of Gold Lake and Gold Bluffs, Slate Range and Sweet Water. Some of them probably made it to the Klondike in '98, for they were a sturdy breed. At the outset of their mining adventures they had been blessed with the vigor of youth and its resilience. They had had the stamina to cope with such harassments as being clawed by grizzlies, struck by rattlesnakes, blown up by premature explosions, buried by cave-ins, dislocated by falling into open mine shafts, racked by scurvy or cholera, dysentery or malarial fever, and shot or knifed in brawls. If they survived these hazards, then the longer they roamed over the hills with pan and pick the more leathery they were. As an old mining camp song put it: "Choose your able-bodied men,/Navvies bold and brawny;/Give them picks and spades, and then/Off to Californy."

The genuine article, as described by a California paper, "feels thoroughly equipped . . . if he possesses a slab of bacon, a few pounds of flour, a little sugar, coffee, tobacco, and an old pick and shovel. If he has a pack animal, all right; if he hasn't, all the same. And thus outfitted he scales the mountains, swims rivers, and skims the plains for months, happy as a stuffed goat." He generally carried a frying pan (if not, a shovel was a good substitute), nearly always brandy or whiskey, and a thirty-dollar butcher knife for picking gold out of rock crevices. His eye distinguished between the splendid white of silver and the bluish-white of lead and zinc; among the pure yellow of gold, the reddish-yellow of copper, and the glitter of fool's gold. An educated nose and tongue identified minerals by smell and taste.

About once a week or oftener reports of rich strikes electrified a mining camp. The stories were generally sensational: of auriferous bars yielding upwards of fifty dollars a day to the hand, a dollar or more to the pan, of rock assaying hundreds of dollars, sometimes thousands, to the ton. A small sackful of dust was enough to raise the emotional temperature, or a chunk of quartz thickly crusted with yellow gold—a fragment that might be, for all anybody knew, the only one of its kind in a whole mine. That possibility seemed unimportant as the camp responded like a runner to the starter's gun, like hunters to the cry of Tally Ho! Immediately the footloose struck their tents, moved out of their brush shanties, abandoned their claims and pushed off, trudging through mud and snow, "with their blankets upon their backs," said one reporter, "as though every moment that is slipping away is a fortune lost."

When the big news got into the local weeklies roundabout, it came out almost according to a routine pattern. First, a few lines mentioned "parties from" or "a gentleman from" the new diggings, who showed the editor specimens of "exceedingly rich" ore. Initially, the tone was perfunctory. But within a few weeks follow-up stories brought in by other parties or by a reporter sent to the scene elaborated upon the prospects in glowing terms that produced items about "Rich Rock," "Struck It," "Made His Pile." Excited correspondents forwarded to the paper long letters full of superlatives that had a snowballing effect. Once an editor started to puff a mining district, he was unlikely to admit later that the place was a humbug or that the ledges had petered out.

Spectacular data on assays, broadcast by the press, bolstered optimism. Dizzying statistics unsettled the mind, aggravated gold fever and induced unrest. Even in a city as large and as detached from the mining scene as San Francisco, alluring tidings of golden harvests awaiting somewhere beyond the horizon made susceptible citizens take to the road. From Marysville, Sacramento, and Stockton, takeoff points for the mines, the exodus was as regular as the equinox, not only of miners, but also of fringe entrepreneurs like shopkeepers, speculators, gamblers, harlots.

There was so much of this frantic movement that a good share of the mining populace seems to have done little more than to scramble fruitlessly from hither to yon. This impression of fluidity that in retrospect appears nervous, like quicksilver, probably derives chiefly from a permanent quota of mobile floaters. Of no settled occupation, these cheerful idlers were always underfoot in established towns like Nevada City and Virginia, and generally drifted into more temporary camps. Hangers-on, like drones in a hive, they were not usually admired, but if they achieved status as "characters," they might merit a friendly, occasionally an affectionate, regard.

Such a one was Old Schimmerhorn, called a "poetical genius" of Gold Hill, Nevada. Supplied with tomatoes, cucumbers, green corn, and corn juice, he was heard to remark gently that "he believed he would go and camp out under a tree." San

Francisco had Uncle Freddy Combs, who dressed like George Washington and who was described as being "as closely shaved as an innocent miner who has submitted his stocks to a San Francisco broker." Pete Mushaway, of Nevada City, enjoyed sitting up with corpses—"a regular funeral sharp," they called him. Old Pike, of Virginia, was so fond of the square meals of the calaboose that when jailed for getting uproariously drunk he would not allow a single day to be deducted from his ten-day sentence. Old Jim Burge, aged 74, of Truckee, got up regularly at five A. M. and started on a cocktail route, visiting four or five bars on the out trip and the same ones in reverse on his return. Then breakfast at his cabin: thick steak, fried potatoes, five fried eggs, coffee with an egg in it and hot roll.

Characters were entertaining, their eccentricities indulgently accepted, but mere bummers had few redeeming traits. They were nuisances, in the way, often in trouble—like John Anderson, a notorious loud-mouthed Copperhead of Gold Hill. When primed with enough free whiskey, he went around town hurrahing for Jeff Davis and cursing all Black Republicans. The authorities finally booted him out.

Editors periodically reproved the shiftless ones but seldom reformed them. "They never," said one paper, "dispute a bill or pay one." A Dutch Flat bummer, accused of lacking energy, replied that he had energy but lacked capital to develop it. A contemplative loafer, surveying his rags and tatters, soliloquized: "People ought to respect me more'n they do, for I'm in holey orders. . . . Whenever anybody treats and says, 'Come, fellars,' I always think my name's 'fellars,' and I've got too good manners to refuse."

Floaters were the undeserving unemployed, who would rather not work if they could avoid it and who preferred to wait for something to turn up. Still, they managed to exist somehow by wheedling food and drinks from open-handed donors—one place was called Loafer Hill—and they made a dependable first wave of stampeders to new diggings. Not burdened with possessions, they could get going fast, but others were not far behind. A big rush, lasting for six months or more, produced the ironical spectacle of late arrivals hurrying into a new district and meeting along the way a large number of the disillusioned shambling out. The disheartened ones had seen the elephant. A dilapidated crowd, they were battered and broke, having failed to strike it rich or to strike much of anything. Perhaps they had been frozen out of claim ownerships or had been unable to handle the labor and expense of blasting, tunneling, crushing the ore, and separating precious metals from resistant quartz.

Such melancholy object lessons, illustrating the difficulties confronting a prospector who was too short of funds to develop a claim, or too lazy, seldom blighted the hopes of eager newcomers or slowed down the shuttling back and forth. "Northern miners," said a California paper, "hurry off south to Big Oak Flat, to the Chowchilla, or Kern River cursing Shasta, Siskiyou and Trinity, and meet southern miners pushing north to Shasta, cursing Oak Flat, Chowchilla, Fresno and the whole d——d southern country."

Editors remonstrated, in tones satirical and serious, against these agitated migrations that hardly ever paid off. In 1851 the San Francisco *Courier* viewed with alarm the disturbing increase in mental breakdowns resulting from anxieties, strong excitements, and frequent disappointments prevalent in a society marked by strain and disorder. Insanity, said the paper, "for some reason, seems to have gained a strong foothold in the State. . . . Word from the mines indicates that the miners are greatly afflicted and that hardly a stage or steamer leaves San Francisco without carrying some sufferer. . . . There is at this time a gentleman in this city who is highly connected in New York, who is now a raving maniac."

Whatever the mental effect of high-toned connections in New York or of high life in San Francisco, it is hard to believe in an epidemic of derangement among those vigorous young men in mining camps. As sound of mind as of wind and limb, they were not commonly given to the worried introspection or sick brooding that forecasts lunatic abnormality. True, the rampant pursuit of fortune created a strained society in which anxieties, excitements, and frustrations were severe enough to drive a man crazy. But it is doubtful that such pressures pushed very many over the edge of sanity. Antidotes for miners' tensions and reverses were the ever-present jug—food might be scarce but not brandy and whiskey—and a saving sense of ironical humor that allowed them to laugh, however wryly, at their predicaments and foibles.

They must have guffawed at their own gullibility as they invented such place names as Sucker Flat, Bunkumville, Dead Broke, Mugginsville, Nary-Red Diggings, Bummerville, Boneyard. They might be disgusted, but they could see the joke without fretting themselves into nervous breakdowns. They were apt at deflating the over-exaggerated accounts of boom towns and lavishly praised mining ground. A prankish correspondent informed an editor of the virtues of a place called Hyfalutinville:

situated in the great country of Nonesuch, on the banks of a beautiful river bearing the melodious Indian name of Siloostreme, which goes roaring to . . . the ocean like those vast streams which flow after a rain through the streets of our principal cities. On either side of the magnificent valley rise two high mountains, soaring heavenward for at least fifty feet. . . . The soil . . . besides its auriferous richness, is well calculated for agricultural purposes, covering the bed rock for at least a foot—in fact almost completely hiding it. . . . The pay dirt is about one hundred feet deep, and is not thought remarkably rich if it does not pay so. . . . The method of working tunnel claims . . . is called the magnetic power; as follows: a live Yankee is placed in the tunnel . . . and such is the *attachment* he has for the precious metal that he will not leave until he is *loaded,* and has to be pulled out. They sometimes die under this process, but your true Yankee thinks nothing of dying once in awhile for money . . . . you will not be surprised when I inform you that in *one month* there has been taken from these diggings something less than $10,000,000!

Some of the boys who rushed off from Poverty Bar to Fraser River in 1858 wrote back that the place was a "sweet-scented humbug," and with derisory humor mentioned the monotonous fare at the Whatcom House: "Soups—Clam and Bean. Roasts [none]. Boil—Clams and Corned Beef. Stews—Clams, Clam Chowder, Clam Pie, Pickled Clams, Fried Clams and Clams Straight. Dessert—Clams with Clam Sauce. Extras—Clams."

The Grass Valley *Union* good-naturedly chaffed "Our Fortune-Hunter." A specimen of a curious species found solely in California, he continually chased gilded bubbles, time and again thought he was about to seize them, yet always they floated airily out of reach or disappeared. Failure after failure only nerved him to greater efforts. "Poor fellow!" said the paper. "Fortune owes him such a debt as we fear she will never pay. The cold world at least owes him a resting place under our mountain pines, and this debt, or in his case, reward, is all the poor fortune-hunter can safely rely on."

Failures were common, often total or nearly so. Dame Shirley (Louise Amelia Knapp Smith Clappe), one of the best chroniclers of California mining life in the early 1850's, records the sad collapse of hopes at Indian Bar. Hundreds of men there had labored for months and spent $3,000 to build a flume to divert a river, expecting a rich cleanup of gold from the gravel. But their slim return for that great outlay in hard work and money was only $41.70. Uncle Zenas, a fictional character from the state of Maine soliloquizing on his own non-success, spoke for many a baffled prospector: "y-a-s, 'tis even *I*, 'Old Zenas,' that's neow in Californy and hain't struck a single *pocket* nor *crevice* yet, and I've traveled e'en a'most as fur as 'tis tew hum."

The Auburn *Placer Herald,* reflecting upon twenty years of stampedes "to distant, dangerous starvation points," irascibly asked whether "one out of every hundred or thousand that have engaged in these wild-goose chases have met with a reward adequate to the toils, risks and sufferings involved." Mrs. A. M.

Shultz, editress of the San Francisco *Hesperian,* tartly inquired: "Why this haste to be rich? Are riches the only good more to be desired than all things else?" The San Francisco *Alta California* remarked with an air annoyed and resigned: "The miners of the Sacramento basin have started out like bees every year during the last decennium, in search of a new abiding place. . . . It seems a serious matter that from 3,000 to 15,000 men should every year leave a State which contains only 120,000 voters; but it is of no avail to grieve about it."

No avail whatever. Editorial protest, solemn or flippant, did not deter anybody from rushing to one new gold field after another. Ironically, editors not only encouraged the prevailing mania by publishing sensational mining news and rumors, but also had been known themselves to succumb to the madness. When the editor of the San Jose *Mercury* took off for the highly praised mining district of White Pine, another paper, anticipating his return after a futile expedition, sketched a graphic word picture of his probable appearance, and in so doing drew a composite portrait of many sanguine prospectors who had vainly sought that will-of-the-wisp, the big thing:

In a few weeks we may expect to behold a seedy individual emerge from the cars at the San Jose depot. His hat will be battered; his beard will be long, matted, a stranger to brush and comb, and full of alkali; his coat will be split down the back, and hang loosely on each side; his knees will act as a gratuitous advertising medium for some first class flouring mill; an old boot, badly out at the toe, will pretend to incase one foot, while an old shoe, run down at the heel, will act as armor for the other; he will carry a roll of dirty blankets tied on his back with bale rope; he will wend his way down the street, an enemy to gas light and praying for darkness; he will not be communicative; he will seek for sympathy. But "Ephraim would be joined to his idols." Let him rip.

These wanderers were animated partly by love of stir and excitement. A community that showed signs of becoming orderly and conventional, of falling into a plodding routine of shopkeepers, hired hands and even white-collar men made independent settlers restive. Chafing under the dullness of emergent respectability, they were eager to push off for uninhabited country where they had more elbow room and fewer restraints.

The primary motive force, however, was the lure of hidden wealth, preferably to be amassed quickly and measured by five or six figures, if not more. Pioneer California experience provided a basis for these expansive notions. In the days of '48 and '49 it was not unusual for a man to wash one hundred ounces of gold a day, worth $16 an ounce. Stories tell of miners shaking gold from bunch grass, and of a market gardener who complained of his poor cabbages but changed his tune when he found gold adhering to the roots. Every fortune-hunter could believe that at any moment he might come upon huge nuggets, perhaps turn up a golden lump as dazzling as the record-breaking find at Carson Hill, weighing 195 pounds and valued at $73,710.

Immigrants who arrived late in the decade after the first fine frenzy had skimmed the cream still thought of mining in the same splendid terms of '49. A good show of color in the pan or surface outcroppings liberally sprinkled with free gold made a man imagine himself a millionaire. A belief common to treasure-seekers, especially among youthful greenhorns, was that they were bound to strike it rich without any effort to speak of. Mark Twain confesses in *Roughing It* that on his toilsome fifteen-day journey to the Humboldt mining district in 1861 he was buoyed up by the certainty that, once there, he would make his pile in a day or two or at most a week merely by picking up a few bushels of loose silver. His chief problem was figuring out the most pleasant ways of spending such a munificent stake. "I expected," he says, "to find masses of silver lying all about the ground. I expected to see it glittering in the sun on the mountain summits."

Possibly he exaggerated, as he often did, yet some fantastic vision of sudden and large returns probably hovered in the imagination of many a prospector, hardbitten though he might be. One journal implied the fantasy in a sarcastic comment upon "adventurers who failed to find mines of twenty dollar gold pieces already coined." A California editor said that whenever old-timers got together, they yarned away to each other over their beer about "the good things they know of the secret places in . . . California. Millions on millions are yet resting in these places, and the indications are that . . . their whereabouts will go down to the grave with the generation who first panned the placers of the Golden State." In the West legends abound of lost mines immensely rich.

Miners' songs exemplified large aspirations: "When I left old New York, to go hunting after gold,/Chunks bigger than my head I could pick up, I was told." One song, set to the tune of "Oh Susannah," rhapsodized about California's rivers that "run on golden beds,/O'er rocks of golden ore,/The valleys six feet deep are said/To hold a plenty more."

Perhaps some of the boys who had seen the elephant may have countered with more pessimistic ditties, many of which described the rugged life of the miner. "He who comes to the mines to find better times,/Had better have tarried in Pike,/For in fifty, I'm told, who are toiling for gold,/There's but one who can count on a strike." Or: "I saw, in dreams, a pile of gold/Its dazzling radiance pour;/No more my visions are of gold,/Alas! my hopes are *ore*." Another lamented: "I've picked and dug, and packed and lugged,/And every honest scheme I've tried on,/Till hunger made me eat at last/The mule I used to ride on." Another pictured the miner laboring "With woolen shirt and rubber boots, in mud up to my knees,/And lice as large as chili beans fighting with the fleas."

A few hours of the wet and back-breaking work of digging, panning, and heaving boulders out of streams dispelled naive faith in easy pickings. In a letter from Douglas Flat in '51, a doctor vividly described his lot: "For five score and ten days he has sojourned in this place—he has dug into the earth—he has dived into the water—he has torn ancient rocks from their resting places, and removed them afar off—he has likewise torn his breeches in parts not to be spoken of!—he has rooted into mud like unto swine!" Fortune, he remarked, was said to smile upon fools, yet when he attempted to seize her, "she glideth off, as though I had caught a hog by his greased tail!"

That experience was common: grueling labor did not, as a rule, unearth great wealth. After 1849 ten to twenty-five cents a pan was considered a good prospect, $5 to $6 a day a satisfactory return. The average daily take was about $2, possibly enough for subsistence but not affluence. Nevertheless, as pell-mell stampedes testify, hard realities could not dispel a lurking conviction that California's golden river beds and valleys just might exist somewhere.

Yet the fortune-hunter's dream reveals something more than amassing gold and silver. In the vision is discernible a yearning for good country, beautiful country, where life could be better than the uncertainties of mining camps. These make-shift communities, short on attractions architectural or social, barren of creature comforts, were generally ugly, crude, sometimes rowdy: canvas-fronted buildings, huts made of calico shirts draped over pine boughs, aboriginal wickiups, tents round and square, plank hovels, a few log cabins. A glass window was a sensation, likely to be sported by a hotel called Empire or Palace or Hotel de Paris. Streets were littered with empty bottles, old boots and hats, sardine cans, oyster tins, ham bones, wornout kettles, broken picks and shovels. The name of one camp, Sublimity, was surely a tongue-in-cheek invention for a so-called town that was some distance short of sublime.

Feminine influence, famous for smoothing rough edges, was slight or non-existent in a predominantly masculine society. One place was called Chivalry Hill, but whether that meant chival-rous behavior or its opposite is anybody's guess; also conjectural are the implications of Ladies Valley and Love-Letter Camp. Dame Shirley, one of two women among a thousand men at In-dian Bar, catalogued a primitive way of life: "no newspapers, no churches, lectures, concerts or theaters; no fresh books, no shopping, calling nor gossiping little tea-drinkings; no parties, no balls, no picnics, no *tableaux,* no charades, no latest fashions, no daily mail (we have an express once a month), no promenades, no rides nor drives; no vegetables but potatoes and onions, no milk, no eggs, no *nothing.*"

Of food, dreary enough to give a dietician the horrors, she also mentioned "hard, salt ham," "poisonous green tea," "quintals of dreadful mackerel fearfully crystallized in black salt" and "barrels upon barrels of rusty pork." Mark Twain, during his three months' stay at Jackass Hill and Angel's Camp in 1864–65, took note of hard beans and dishwater coffee for breakfast, dishwater and beans for dinner, both warmed up for supper, and four kinds of soup: Hell-fire, General Debility, Insanity, and Sudden Death. "But when they talk of cooking," runs one miner's song, "I'm mighty hard to beat—/I've made ten thousand loaves of bread the d——l could not eat."

The inhabitants of a camp were a sun-browned lot armed with pistols and bowie knives, a shaggy crew slouch-hatted, booted, long-haired, often luxuriantly bearded and so profane that, as Dame Shirley remarked, "people who never uttered an oath in their lives in the 'States,' now 'clothe themselves with curses as with a garment.' " The image was formidable, yet these men, though not inclined to be docile, were roughly good-natured, cheerful, hospitable and companionable, adept at telling tall tales, and fond of listening to other good yarn-spinners.

Every camp had its loafers, who never had enough money to get very drunk and who were always in debt for board and whiskey. Alonzo Delano, "Old Block," in "The Idle and the Industrious Miner" (1854) drew contrasting word pictures: first of the sober citizen who was always up at dawn to work his claim, and who observed the Sabbath by dutifully reading his Bible. On Sunday also the industrious man washed clothes, darned socks, covered rents in his pants with flour sack patches, taped his boots, sharpened his pick, chopped a week's firewood, wrote letters to his family back in the States, baked bread, and boiled enough beans and pork to last awhile.

Whereas the idle miner was a disreputable sluggard who wasted the morning in bed, and who neglected household chores. He was one who could sing: "I never changed my fancy shirt, the one I wore away,/Until it got so rotten I finally had to say,/'Farewell, old standing collar, in all thy pride of starch,/I've worn thee from December till the seventeenth of March.' " On Sunday the backslider joined the noisy crowd that made the Sabbath hideous with horse-racing, cock-fighting, and brawls. He toured the saloons and hung around gambling dens, where he boozily staked his last dollar on a losing card. Laziness led to thievery that forced him to flee to escape hanging. Then he stabbed a man and ended up in jail: such a fate, according to Old Block, was the inevitable wage of slothfulness.

How many of those blue- and red-shirted fellows were faithful Bible-readers can only be surmised. One place name was Gospel Gulch and another was Piety Hill, but they suggest the irony of ebullient young men more devilish than pious. At any rate, Bible notwithstanding, even the reasonably well behaved miner broke down occasionally and the whole camp took to the bottle until everybody was laid out. Dame Shirley tells of a four-day carouse at Christmas, when the boys danced, then collapsed in heaps, howling, barking and roaring, some in "that transcendental state of intoxication, when a man is compelled to hold on to the earth for fear of falling off."

J. D. Borthwick, an Englishman who spent three years in the mines, writes of an ex-sailor who spent $400 on a glorious spree that went on for a week: "most affectionately and confidentially drunk in the forenoon, fighting drunk in the afternoon, and dead drunk at night." A horrified observer in 1858 bewailed the dreadful intemperance of mining camps. "Drunk, drunk," he moaned, "—go where you may, every little town is infested with groggeries and drunkards. . . . thousands of young men are growing old . . . in vice and dissipation. . . . There is no such thing as society in the mining regions; any drunken set of blackguards who have money can rule those who pretend to decency. There is no restraint, and no example but that of rudeness, and of a degrading tendency."

Get drunk they certainly did on brandy straight at $20 a bottle, one ounce of dust ($16) for a tincup full, on brandy punch, brandy sling, whiskey, gin cocktails, claret, even champagne. Drinks were often as elaborately concocted, with the aid of expensive canned fruit, as in the most sophisticated bars of San Francisco. According to Dame Shirley, "there is no possible luxury connected with drinking, which is procurable in California, that cannot be found in the mines." The frugal fellow who saved money by baking his own bread thought nothing of blowing his day's take at a saloon or monte table. If he had a run of good luck, struck a pocket perhaps and made a stake, he was likely to take off for a high old time in Sacramento or San Francisco, returning after a while stony broke and bedraggled but ready to do it again.

Yet any wholesale condemnation of mining camp morals and morale is too sweeping to be universally true. On those points testimony is mixed. There is the reminiscence of the veteran who was delighted with the beauty of the California country. "I thought it was a kind of heaven," he said, "but it ain't though. . . . It's a sight more like *t'other place*, which we don't care to see! . . . Lying, stealing, cheating, swearing, drinking, gambling, horse-racing, cock-fighting, Sabbath-breaking, forging, counterfeiting, murdering—all sorts of sin . . . I declare, I never!" A Grass Valley editor, reprehending the barroom rowdyism of irresponsible citizens, deplored "the vice, temptation and recklessness of California society."

On the other hand, a native of Omega remarked upon "the most peaceable and gentlemanly set of miners to be found anywhere; quarrels of any sort are very rare, and differences . . . are generally concluded by the . . . rational plan of reference and arbitration." The men of Happy Camp may also have been inclined, more or less, to peaceful co-existence. Dame Shirley did not look upon Indian Bar as merely an unrestrained hell-hole, nor did she feel degraded by the roughness of her surroundings. Once, at least, this refined and civilized eastern lady tried panning gold herself. "I wet my feet," she said, "tore my dress, spoilt a pair of new gloves, nearly froze my fingers, got an awful headache, took cold and lost a valuable breastpin." But she must have enjoyed the excitement of seeing the color because she kept at it long enough to pan out $3.25. When mining petered out at Indian Bar and the camp disintegrated, she had become so attached to the place that she was reluctant to leave.

She was fond of it despite daily evidence that a mining town was not as placid as a quiet New England village. There were conflicts between the law-abiding and the lawless, racial clashes involving Mexicans, Spaniards, and Chinese, occasionally gun play and knifing. To show that blackguards were not all-powerful, however, law-and-order men swiftly liquidated sluice robbers, sometimes ejected chronic trouble-makers, and now and then staged impromptu hangings of other undesirable citizens.

In a society that, at its best, was more turbulent than stable, it is not surprising that the gold-seeker's dream had overtones of the recurrent human search for perfection, for lost Eden, for Utopia, or at any rate for a place where the wanderer could imagine himself settling down to enjoy domestic bliss in peace and comfort. Farm boys from Missouri and Iowa dreamed of good grass country for pasturing beef cattle and milk cows. They had an eye for fertile crop land where they could set out fruit trees, raise potatoes and carrots, grain, garden sass. This attraction to the soil was so strong that a good many transplanted farmers eventually gave up mining to become California ranchers.

In the gold-hunter's makeup was a vein of sentiment verging on sentimentality, yet he was a practical man, too, as well as a homespun philosopher who was not hostile to the culture of his time. Miners flocked to theaters in foothill towns to see Edwin Booth, Lotta Crabtree, Lola Montez and others, showing admiration for a favorite actress or singer by tossing a shower of nuggets upon the stage. Not all places were quite so primitive as the camp described by Dame Shirley. Lecture lyceums were common, as well as literary and debating societies. Artemus Ward, Prentice Mulford, and Mark Twain all lectured in mining camps.

Miners were neither ignorant nor illiterate. Old Block said that he found more honesty and intelligence, more scientific and literary knowledge among those uncouth-looking fellows than he had seen elsewhere. They were great readers who read whatever was at hand, passing around old newspapers until they were worn to tatters. When the most famous West Coast weekly, the San Francisco *Golden Era,* began in 1852 as "A Good Family Paper, Calculated for circulation in every parlor and miner's cabin," it soon acquired over a thousand subscribers in the northern mines. The *Pioneer,* a monthly founded in 1854, was so popular that when an expressman delivered a bundle of copies at a town, they were immediately picked up by miners in nearby camps, then went the rounds from cabin to cabin. The *Wide West* was another favorite: "A Weekly Newspaper Devoted to Literature, the Arts, and the Diffusion of General Intelligence."

What the miners liked, and readers generally, was homily and exposition—"Last Moments of Washington," "The Agriculture of Palestine," "Recipe for Happiness," "Dignity of Vocation," and so on—and in narrative plenty of sentiment, heavy romance, melodrama. Consider these fiction titles of the 1850's: "The Dice of Death; or, The Last Wager"; "Maritana, the Wild Maid of Montcalm; or, The Grotto of the Infernal Shaft"; "The Fearful Messenger; or, The Sailor's Doom"; "Madeline: The Heartless"; "Woman's Revenge."

There was a good deal of verse, every small town paper publishing at least one poem per issue, sometimes more. Poets and would-be poets celebrated the rapture and the heartache of love, the beauties of nature, the rewards of sobriety and industry and so forth in an artificial style imitative of Byron, Hood, Thomas Moore, and Mrs. Hemans—"Where is Our Boy To-Night?" "Granny's Chair," "The Withered Daisies," "Woman's Tears," "Look on the Bright Side," "Heart Thoughts," and many others of that genre. The tone was self-consciously literary, like this: ' "Twas evening's hour; the light and fleecy clouds/That softly floated on the zephyr's breath/Were blushing crimson, 'neath the ardent kiss/The Day-God gave. . . ." Stilted conceits were the stock in trade of contemporary versifiers and frequently of prose writers as well: "hie to some sequestered spot where flowers spring up unbidden, bloom and die ungathered; where the tiny rill babbles its never ending song of glee, and the quiet shades are eloquent of nature's poesy."

An affected, anemic sort of writing it was, alien to the robust West, yet the ornate and mawkish evidently went down very well in mining regions. Bret Harte's poem, "Dickens in Camp," tells of a miner who drew from his pack "a hoarded volume" and read the lachrymose story of Little Nell to his comrades around the camp fire. Silence fell from pine and cedar, fir trees listened, haggard faces lost their careworn look "And cards were dropped from hands of listless leisure/To hear the tale anew." The episode is fictitious, yet the implications seem genuine. Harte had first-hand knowledge of mining camps. As a city man, something of a dude, he appears not to have felt at ease in mining country or ever to have been whole-heartedly western in spirit, but he must have had some inkling of sentimentality in the miner's character. Old timers' reminiscences recall the camp fire and the story-teller who enthralled his listeners. "With what emphasis," says one recollection, "did he articulate each syllable and word as he unfolded the web of Fact or Fancy in which it was his design to enmesh us."

Verse and prose often described in affecting language the plight of the lonesome prospector bereft of wife or sweetheart left behind on the old home place hundreds of miles away, part of a past that seemed ages distant. Confronting a drab life of drudgery and beans, observing the lamentable disrepair of his ragged clothes, he mused upon the time when he had cut a dash as a dandy in the height of fashion. He thought of the pleasures he had casually given up: clean linen, clean white sheets, girls to spark, and especially food various and plentiful. A gloomy song reflected on the good old days "When all the girls loved me" and in a mood of extravagant romancing went on to say that "They washed and cooked for me." Out in the mountains, alas, "I wash and cook myself,/I never more shall cut a swell,/But here must dig for pelf."

The poor fellow might have gone back any time had pride not prevented him from returning empty-handed and thus confirming home town opinion that he was a fool for having set out in the first place. So he kept on digging, spurred by the hope that the next thrust of the shovel would turn up unbelievable riches. The author of "The Miner's Ten Commandments" added an eleventh, which directed the fortune-hunter always to remember wife and children and to turn homeward when he could say: "I have enough—God bless them—I will return." Not many, apparently, reached that point. Hence, they cheered when they received letters from back there, drooped when they got none and sang dolorous songs like "I'm Sad and Lonely Here," "Home of My Boyhood," "The Girl I Left Behind Me," and "Do They Miss Me at Home?" An editor remarked upon "The Five H's.— Five of the sweetest words in the English language begin with H—Heart, Hope, Home, Happiness and Heaven." A ribald fellow journalist marred the touching effect by a postscript: "We'll add another—Hot whiskey punch."

"Home!" exclaimed an amateur writer on the Mother Lode:

oh what a thought to a lonely, disconsolate, disheartened miner, who has toiled for years in the gulches and ravines of the California mountains, and has met bitter disappointment in all his labor. The very thoughts of "home" sink deep into his soul. . . . Oh, how he would like to hear the murmur of the gentle rivulet that warbles past his cottage door at "home." Oh, how he would like to see once more the partner of his bosom, who . . . would fly with open arms to embrace him . . . and how the little children at home would cling around him to be dandled on father's knee and receive with grateful little hearts a father's smile and a father's kiss. But while amongst the foot hills of the Sierra Nevada, no such sounds or pleasures greet him on his return from ransacking the bowels of the earth. . . . Home, sweet home, with all thy peaceful charms, how he longs to see thee and never roam from thy pleasant shades again.

Nostalgia, a constant theme, probably inspired such place names as Michigan Bluff and Michigan Bar, Missouri Bar, Iowa Hill, Alleghany. The haunting memory of things past offset the rugged and earthy in a mining district with touches of the fanciful and romantic. One camp was called Jenny Lind, after the famous Swedish Nightingale; another after Lew Wallace's hero, Ben Hur; another epitomized the mysterious East in the poetic name of Cathay. Among mines and mining companies were May Boy, George Washington, Warbler, Silver Cord, Beethoven, William Shakespeare. There was lyrical beauty in euphonious Spanish names like Mariposa, the butterfly; Vallecito, the little valley; Hornitos, the little ovens of Mexican adobe burial mounds; Melones, where the gold looked like melon seeds.

All of that shows imagination and sensitivity. But if romanticism was a part of the miner's character, it was subordinate to the primary urge. When the dreamer found pleasing country that somewhat resembled his dream world, he did not hesitate to destroy its beauty in a furious effort to get the gold. He dug, blasted, sluiced, turned streams out of their beds, tore up the earth. He ravaged forests, pasture lands and the crops of ranchers, who were powerless to protect themselves. The gold-seeker was as destructive as a bulldozer. "The typical American miner," said a California editor, "would tear up the streets of Pandemonium if by so doing he could get ten cents to the pan, and about the only chance for him to get to Heaven is to start a gold excitement up there."

For almost forty years the dominance of mining over all other enterprises allowed prospectors to stake claims anywhere, in the center of a town or of a vineyard, on anybody's supposedly private property. If gold were found in the middle of a hay field, the ground was so promptly claimed by miners that the owner might be dispossessed of his own acres. In Como, Nevada, when it was discovered that the Como Brewery was built directly over a blind lead, a company immediately sank a shaft in the cellar. The claim was appropriately named Lager Beer Ledge. In Virginia, the Potosi Mining Company once ordered property owners on B, C and D Streets to vacate as the company claimed the ground. In San Francisco, when somebody picked up a piece of virgin gold on a vacant lot, twenty prospectors were on the scene within an hour, digging, panning and getting their boots full of water.

Most devastating of all methods was hydraulic mining. Powerful streams of water, erupting under high pressure from huge nozzles, eroded hills, wrecked roads, undermined buildings, clogged streams with debris that also covered grazing lands below, and obliterated whole towns. An editor satirically recorded the destruction of Cayoteville: "the ruthless power of water, under a 200-foot pressure . . . sapped the foundations of the city. Gradually . . . it has melted away . . . and its inhabitants have folded their tents and silently stolen away. Pompeii, Herculaneum, Ninevah and Babylon, have all left behind them visible attestations of former splendor—but Cayoteville has disappeared forever, and not a solitary ruin marks the spot where it once existed in imperial magnificence. *Sic transit gloria mundi.*" Scars of tremendous man-made erosions still remain in California, though less raw now after the lapse of a century.

Because the miner did not lose sight of his main objective, his dream, like all dreams, was confused or contradictory and he himself a paradox of clashing impulses. A Washoe reporter on the Gold Hill *News* described the fortune-hunter's vision when he wrote about "The 'Big Thing'—What and Where It Is":

Just now the restless . . . portion of our population appear to be a little undecided in regard to the exact location of the "big thing" —the big thing *par excellence*. . . . But, notwithstanding that they don't know exactly where it is, they are all going after it—about the 1st of April. A great many dream of a sort of *terra incognita*. . . . Here they love to imagine huge veins projecting from the hills, all bright and glittering with native gold and silver. Of course, they fix up . . . all the surroundings to suit. They have streams for running mills, each skirted by a meadow of luxuriant clover and grass; springs bubbling up in the ravines, wood growing on the hills, and everything as convenient as the heart could wish. This is as they see the unknown land in their dreams, and they continue to dream of this paradise . . . till it seems a reality and not a Dorado of their own creation—made of the "baseless fabric" of all visions. They come at last to the firm belief in the existence of what at first they merely imagined might be—their hearts swell to behold and tread these wilds in whose paths no miner's foot ever left its print. An outfit is obtained and away they go, over rugged mountains, across arid, alkali deserts, on and on—never stopping—never discouraged—in search of the golden gardens of their dreams—after the "big thing."

Irony runs through that exposition and pathos, too. Implicit in the lines are the manifold disappointments of hope deferred, of the collapse of visions that are composed of the baseless fabric of chimeras. The big thing was as elusive, and as magnetic, as the end of the rainbow. Evidence of the pursuit appears today in the remnants of many California camps. "In the hollows, grown over with blossoming vines," says one historian, "are acres upon acres of boulders and debris, moved, sifted, and piled up by the hands of pioneers. . . . Once this was Red Dog Camp, or Mad Mule Gulch, or Murderer's Bar; now it is only a nameless canyon, the counterpart of hundreds of others . . . each one of them all once full to the brim and overflowing with noisy, beating, rushing, roaring, masculine life."

# 2

**XXXXXXXXXX**

# Excelsior

WHEN the Gold Hill man wrote about "The Big Thing" early in 1864, some Mother Lode camps had already become ghost towns, but there was nothing shadowy or ghostlike about the perennial search for *terra incognita*. In the spring of 1864 stupendous news was in the making about a new gold district called Excelsior. It was to cause one of the wildest of all stampedes. But this place, unlike others that had stirred up gold excitements, did not drop out of sight after a mad rush of fortune-hunters and a few months of furore. It was destined to hold the attention of mining men for almost a hundred years thereafter. Until well along in the twentieth century Excelsior—or, as it came to be called, the Meadow Lake district—was consistently in western mining news as a provocative source of great wealth. Perhaps even today the story is still unfinished.

This country was in the eastern half of Nevada County, California, one of the richest gold-producing sections of the state. A region about fifty miles square, at a mean altitude of 7,000 feet on the westerly slope of the Sierra Nevada, Excelsior lay between the Henness Pass and Dutch Flat routes to Washoe, forty miles from Nevada City and something over sixty miles from Virginia. Heaton's station was a point of entry, Polley's and Webber's stations not far away, Jackson's Ranch nearby. Just over the county line eight miles to the south was the town of Cisco that within a few years would be the eastern terminus of the Central Pacific Railroad.

Winters were long and severe, summers short but delightful. Beautiful valleys of luxuriant grass, dotted with wildflowers, were watered by meandering willow-fringed streams that united to form an upper tributary of the South Yuba River. Pasturage was so lush that a rancher there later advertised for farm animals to board at $3 a month: "Poore leane hungry horses mules and cattle eats loots of grass, and so does a poor hungry jackass. Having best quality grass clover and timothy up to a jackass in Fordyce Valley am prepared to weather bord from one to (500) Five Hundred Frames of the above descriptive animals . . . . Enquire Undersigned his Hous Meadow Lake dam Valley. Jerome Fordyce." Grass up to a jackass was the right way to put it.

Massive ridges of granite, snow-covered until midsummer, marched grandly across the landscape, the prevailing tone of light gray looking austere and ashen. Their lower slopes, heavily timbered with digger pine, fir, black oak, and tamarack, were a solid dark green, somber and magnificent. Dominating the scene was Old Man Mountain, a majestic sentinel of 7,789 feet. An observer described him as a "huge old, rough mass of solid granite, so prominent from every portion of the surrounding country. . . . a hoary headed, case hardened old fellow, surely, who has stood through all eternal ages, glowering down in rugged grandeur and lofty regard upon the smaller hills and mountains around."

From the Old Man's summit the view was panoramic. To the east a great jumble of snowy crags crossed the Divide at 10,000 feet; far to the north were the stern walls of the Downieville Buttes. Westward the eye followed river courses—Feather, Yuba, Sacramento, American—and foothills that stretched for fifty miles toward the Pacific until they flattened out in the distant immensity of the San Joaquin and Sacramento valleys, the Coast Range looming dimly beyond. The Sierra Nevada was known as the Alps of California.

In a shallow draw near the county line on the north was Meadow Lake, about a mile long by three-quarters wide. This

Meadow Lake and Dam. July, 1893. Lake nearly covered with ice and snow.

*Bancroft Library, University of California, Berkeley.*

body of water, a visitor said, was "the most beautiful lake that the eye ever beheld . . . spreads itself like a sheet of silver." It was flanked, as the name implied, by gently sloping meadow thick with grass and bordered by heavy stands of pine and cedar. Two miles south and lower by a thousand feet was the larger Fordyce Lake. Both were deep, clear and cold. In the region were Phoenix Lake, Old Man Lake, Lake Pepin, French Lake and some thirty others, besides any number of icy mountain pools fed by melting snow.

On the hard granite of the mountains were a great many gold-bearing ledges anywhere from two feet to eight feet thick or more, the rock dark red, almost black. Different from the usual well-defined quartz outcroppings that stood out boldly and were readily detected by the experienced miner, those of the Excelsior district were not easily visible to the naked eye. Once the broad dark stains had been observed, however, they were sometimes traceable for a considerable distance. Veins near Old Man Mountain could be followed for half a mile or more. Close inspection revealed thin flakes of free gold in the spongy decomposed rock on the surface.

Here in one locality were all the requirements of the visionary's paradise, in addition to other assets he had not thought of: beauty, grandeur, fertile grass land, bracing climate, dense forests promising plenty of wood, an abundance of water, level terrain for town sites—even, as a reporter later noted, dying snowbanks in August, "so that the sports . . . and those that like sherry cobblers in warm weather, need not lack the wherewithal to cool them with, obtainable within a short distance." Above all, was the indispensable attraction: apparently a vast quantity of gold. The place seemed like a fortune-hunter's dream come true. Verily, it looked like the big thing *par excellence*.

If the high Sierra country of Excelsior was not literally an untrodden wilderness, it was almost so. Not many human beings had set foot in those parts. In 1857 the South Yuba Water Company sent in a construction gang to build a dam across a small tributary of the South Yuba River, the purpose being to furnish water to miners and towns in the southwestern part of Nevada County. The granite structure, 1,150 feet long, 42 feet high and 15 feet wide at the apex, impounded Meadow Lake. Although the men were there for months, many of them old hands at prospecting, they did not look for treasure because of a fixed belief, long-standing in California, that gold never occurred in granite. Besides, the Excelsior ledges were inconspicuous, sometimes obscured by the gloom of forests and covered by piles of boulders. So when the dam-builders had finished their job, they departed without having disturbed very much the peace of this mountain fastness or its four-footed fauna.

The discoverer of gold in the Excelsior district was Henry H. Hartley. Born in East Berlin, Adams County, Pennsylvania, in 1834, he had been a precocious child fond of books, later becoming a competent linguist who had a speaking knowledge of several foreign languages. Possessed of an inquiring mind and the countryman's ability to turn his hand to a variety of manual crafts, he was also a person of refinement and great strength of character. These commendable qualities, reinforced by intelligence and resourcefulness, made him an admirable example of the best kind of versatile young men attracted by the promise of the Far West.

Joining the overland surge toward the Pacific, probably in the mid-1850's, he stopped off for a few years with a sister in Iowa, where he clerked in a bookstore. Then, about 1860, he went on to California. Having a kinsman named Frank Picking in Dutch Flat, Hartley set out for that town, and not long after he arrived there he was exploring country around the headwaters of Bear River in Placer County. An adventurous sort who relished the solitude of primitive regions, he then tramped northeastward some fifteen miles or so into the mountains of Nevada County, where he built a cabin against a hill near Meadow Lake.

As he told the story more than twenty-five years later, he built on the windward side of the hill, then spent much of the first winter in a prolonged tussle with the weather. An early snow drifted against the cabin; the next one, heavier, covered it. He dug himself out and lengthened the front porch to make one end of the place extend beyond drifts. He also made his chimney higher, but another snowfall necessitated further extension of both porch and chimney. Off and on all winter, he said, he made these additions until, when spring came and the snow melted off, his cabin looked like a right-angled triangle with one side caved in. He maintained that his porch was 1,200 feet long, his chimney so high that he could see the top of it only on a clear day. That was his story. Evidently he became enough of a westerner to learn the technique of the tall tale. Before the next winter descended upon him he built a cabin on the other side of the hill.

A loner who was well suited to the life of a hermit, he flourished on the hard winters of the Sierras, earning a livelihood by trapping mink, martin, coyotes, red and silver foxes, the more rare and highly prized black fox, bear and otter. He ranged from the northern end of Lake Tahoe to the meridian of the Downieville Buttes, making the rounds of traps on skis, called Norwegian snowshoes. Sometimes out for days, he set up way stations at convenient points for camping overnight. He became an expert skier, agile footwork often saving him from encounters with short-tempered grizzlies and from the dangers of the deadly avalanche.

Like Thoreau, who now and then emerged from his Walden Pond retreat to see what was going on in the town of Concord, Hartley occasionally snowshoed down to Cisco, where he spent a few days. In Bob Campbell's combination hotel-store-bar he discussed ponderous questions with railroad surveyors and others gathered around the stove. One who was there recalls, also, that Hartley "would saw on an old fiddle and create a noise that did have some effect in soothing the savages." He was an adjustable fellow, fond of living alone, certainly no effusive extrovert, yet not disdainful of human society.

When not on the trail he worked on his pelts, converting them into valuable furs. An ingenious craftsman, he fashioned gloves from leftover odds and ends, also caps and victorines that were much admired by ladies of Placerville, Nevada City and other towns. In early summer he carried his furs below to the Sacramento valley, where he sold them, then tarried for a number of weeks while he stocked up on provisions and other supplies, these including no doubt books and periodicals for reading in off-duty moments. By the time of the first snowfall, September or thereabouts, he was back in the mountains again.

For several years he followed this rigorous and self-reliant routine. Not being an experienced prospector, he made no special effort to find gold, although he had noticed the dark reddish-brown stuff streaking the granite. Then, in June, 1863, casually beating one stone against another, he shelled out a number of small yellow flakes—*chispas*, they are called. He seems not to have been agitated by the usual high fever of the typical gold-seeker, but the show of color had the customary effect of heightening the interest and quickening the pulse. When he returned from the valley in August, he brought with him two other men, John Simons and Henry Feutel, and all three began prospecting in earnest.

In September of that year they organized the Excelsior Company and staked off 2,000 feet on each of two parallel ledges some seventy feet apart, named Union No. 1 and No. 2, about a mile south of Meadow Lake. When they started to work these claims, mining began in the Excelsior district.

But nobody paid much attention to what Hartley and his friends were doing, nor did they inform the papers. The place was so remote that they were not pestered by inquisitive reporters. Word got around, however, for in 1864 another outfit, the California Company, claimed 1,700 feet on each of four ledges called California, Knickerbocker, Indian Boy, and Indian Queen. Yet this company caused no particular stir either, and stories of gold strikes in the high Sierras did not get into the news for six months or more.

# 3

✕✕✕✕✕✕✕✕✕✕✕

# Gold Rush 1865

IN THE SPRING of 1865 rumors of ledges loaded with gold in the mountains of Nevada County began to float into other parts of California and over the line into the state of Nevada. One of the places most receptive to these tidings was Virginia City. Times were dull there. Mining on the Comstock was showing signs of failure, and other diggings that had sent the boys pelting off now and then—Humboldt, Reese River, Esmeralda—were played out. Washoe citizens were in a mood ripe for new adventures.

On June 6, under the heading "Rich Croppings," the Virginia *Union* told of specimens from the Knickerbocker ledge "filled with native gold and black sulphurets of silver." The next day the Gold Hill *News*, just over the Divide, said that "The Excelsior Company have prospected their ledge by means of cross cuts and shafts, which show the ledge to be about fifty feet wide, and enormously rich in gold." On June 10 the *News* reported that croppings from the Excelsior district "have been assayed which went as high as $954." On the 14th the Virginia *Union*, in a story entitled "Exceedingly Rich," said that "a couple of gentlemen" had brought in "some very rich specimens of gold and silver bearing rock, which fully equal if not surpass anything we have heretofore seen. . . . In all the specimens native gold and silver could be plainly seen . . . and an assay shown us went some $55,000 to the ton—gold and silver."

Reports traveled to Dutch Flat, Nevada City, Grass Valley, San Francisco, losing nothing of their appeal by repetition of gaudy data on large ledges and sensational assays. Additional items crept in from time to time, like panning dirt at 25¢ to $4 to the pan. One editor said: "specimens shown to us are so filled with gold as to suggest the idea that they had been sprinkled with bronze. . . . in a few months we have no doubt there will be a town as large as Nevada almost upon the summit of the Sierras." Another concluded: "This new mining district . . . is evidently destined to become celebrated. . . . We are satisfied that California still holds out the best prospects for the miner, and that it is a waste of time to roam over . . . Idaho and Montana to look for gold."

The news was irresistible. It worked the same compulsive magic that had cast its spell many times before. By the middle of June, nimble-footed gold-hunters had set out from Virginia and elsewhere. Machinery for four quartz mills was reported to be on the way to the Excelsior district, "the owners having satisfied themselves," one paper said, "that the rock taken out from these claims will pay more than many of the best claims in the Washoe country." By what blend of fact, fancy, and will-to-believe they had satisfied themlselves was not revealed, but off they put. In the new diggings ten sites for stamp mills and sawmills had been taken up, and energetic fellows were clearing ground for the erection of mill buildings. Robinson and Mc-Cartney planned a 20-stamp mill, and Captain William Kidd, a Virginia banker, had similar ideas.

On the scene great excitement gripped everybody. By July some 250 men were already there, also about twenty women, their numbers continually augmented by others rushing in at the rate of some fifty a day. Prospectors scurried about staking claims, every claim, one optimist said, "being actively worked, all having the greatest confidence in the great wealth of the ledges, which will undoubtedly pay from the surface down, for the croppings assay from $9,000 to $61,000 to the ton. The lowest assay yet obtained is $65 to the ton."

There were only a few cabins in gulches, no town as yet, men camping out anywhere. A sharp climate, pleasantly sunny during the day, did not call for weather-tight shelter or much warmth, although a one-inch snowfall in July temporarily damaged the illusion of a summer resort. At that altitude nights were brisk, but a man could roll up in his blankets, if he had any. Impressionable men had an eye for the beauty of Meadow Lake, silvery in the sun, deep blue in some lights, set off against bordering masses of dark green fir and cedar. Said one: "The town site and the surrounding scenery is . . . the finest that I have ever seen in this or any other country. . . . no pen could more than do it justice, even were it handled by the hand of a poet."

In the main, however, immigrants had not come merely to admire the view. They spent most of their time looking for gold, whole platoons clambering among boulders and tramping through timber searching for likely prospects. One letter-writer said that, surveying the country from a high knoll, he saw so many creatures crawling among the trees that he thought the woods were full of bears, "but when the dark object comes closer you will find it to be a quartz hunter, a small magnifying glass in his hand, a handkerchief before his left eye so as to save the trouble of closing it a thousand times an hour. Every pocket is full of rocks, and thus does he walk up and down hill. Here are good indications—out comes pen, ink and paper, and a large notice is drawn up, claiming all dips, spurs, angles, and variations, and runs all over creation. . . . Some even have printed notices, drawn up by an attorney."

Within six weeks after the news appeared in the papers, the entire five miles of the main ledge had been staked off and a good deal more besides. Any pile of boulders that bore the slightest resemblance to a ledge was likely to be somebody's claim, the location duly filed with the Recorder of Nevada County under a fancy name like Lady Adams, Gem, Golden Spur, Hidden Treasure, Lucky Boy, Shooting Star, Gently Glide, Prairie Flower.

Every patch of timber was taken up either by speculators or by sawmill and mining companies: Washington, Rattlesnake, North American, Yellow Jacket, Potosi, Crow Driver, Monitor, and many others—all of them reportedly engaged in a great commotion of sinking shafts and tunneling. Excelsior mining shares were quoted in Virginia at $10 to $100 a foot. Henry Mayer, a Virginia assayer, arrived with a German expert to open an assay office, which at once did a booming business. The place throve on assays; they were its staff of life. W. J. Organ and R. G. Tibbetts organized a pony express to carry mail and newspapers three times a week to and from Nevada City. Several Washoe butchers had set up shop, a hotel of sorts was called the Howard House, and two saloons slaked thirsts with brandy and whiskey praised for strength but not for quality. "One 'horn,'" said a patron, "will 'capture' a man."

Dozens of industrious letter-writers sent long missives to hometown papers, full of details about the country, its ledges, and its people: mining data by the column, human interest stories, minor news items, chatty gossip, humor and satire. Probably no other mining district, with the possible exception of the Comstock, had ever been so thoroughly described and discussed, so fully explained and analyzed. Intense publicity gave the impression, particularly to people unfamiliar with the difficulties up there at the summit, that the district had miraculously become a going concern overnight, complete with all accessories necessary for getting out gold at once. The reality was not like that, but affairs did move.

In late June a town site of 160 acres was laid off by A. C. "Alex" Wightman, a Virginia broker who was from the start a leading citizen of the new district, and Charley Parker, formerly of the Virginia *Bulletin*. Surveyed by J. A. Brumsey, a civil engineer from Crystal Peak, the spot chosen was on the south-west shore of Meadow Lake on property owned by the California Company. It was a beautiful location, "the prettiest site for a city," said a visitor, "—a summer city—that I have ever seen in California."

This community originated in a manner unusual, if not unique, among mining towns. It did not grow haphazardly as a straggling array of shacks and cabins meandering helter-skelter wherever inhabitants took a fancy to put them up. On the contrary, this town took shape according to a plan presumably evolved by Wightman, Brumsey, Parker, representatives of the California Company like J. K. Stuart and Eric Prahm, and perhaps other interested parties.

They platted spacious streets eighty feet wide, intersecting at right angles, named A, B, C one way, First, Second, Third the other. Blocks were divided into lots of sixty-foot frontage, eighty-foot depth, a sixteen-foot alleyway running through the middle of each block. A portion of the lakeside end on the north, 300 feet square, was reserved for a Plaza. Surely no other gold town had been conceived with so much forethought. For the time being it was generally called Summit City. Corner lots sold at first for $25, provided buyers agreed to start building within fourteen days, middle lots free under the same condition. During the next few weeks, however, the demand became so pressing that the giveaway ceased, and the price of choice lots shot up to $400 or more.

It is not clear what provisions were made for town government. There were no municipal officers, no sheriff, no police force, although a man named W. Smith was appointed night watchman, evidently a sort of constable. By late summer a deputy sheriff, I. E. Brokaw, was on duty, also a Justice of the Peace. Apparently town matters requiring action were to be handled by the traditional California method, in force in mining camps since the early 1850's, of calling an assembly of claim owners, hearing their opinions, and taking a vote.

Henry Hartley, the only begetter of the whole place, seems to have taken no conspicuous part in launching the community. Not an organization man, he was never prominent in town affairs, governmental or social, yet he continued to live in the district, probably in the same old trapper's cabin. No longer a trapper, however, he worked his claims unobtrusively, not noisily boasting about the wealth of his property but making a comfortable living.

A miners' meeting in mid-July adopted the 1852 mining laws of Nevada County, resolved that the diggings be called the Meadow Lake district, and defined its boundaries: "Commencing at Culbert's Bridge, on the South Yuba, thence to the head waters of Bear River; thence along the County line of Placer and Nevada, to its intersection with the State line; thence along the State line to the intersection of the County line of Sierra and Nevada; thence along the said County line to the head waters of the South Branch of the Middle Yuba River, from thence in a southerly course to place of beginning." The good sense of these proceedings is commendable. If many new inhabitants were distracted by gold fever, among them were enough responsible men of sober judgment to lay the foundations for a stable society.

For a while, pending the completion of permanent buildings, the "City" had the miscellaneous look of tents and brush shanties that reminded old-timers of the camps of '49. But it took on a more orderly appearance as the pace accelerated throughout the summer. Enthusiastic promoters laid out three other towns—Richport, Wightman's Camp (later called Baltimore City), Lakeville—and by the middle of August newcomers were surging into the district at the rate of a hundred a day.

Getting to the Meadow Lake country was no easy matter. From Virginia the usual way was over a rough road sixty miles to the junction of the Henness Pass and Donner Lake routes, then taking another stage to Summit City. Immigrants from the west could ride the stage to Jones' station, twenty-five miles east of Dutch Flat, and from there take to the saddle or leg it in on foot.

Whatever route the traveler followed, he could count on being squeezed into a jam-packed coach, then being violently jolted up for a day or two by bouncing over rocky roads and banging against stumps on twisting trails that were scarcely more than wheel tracks through wilderness. Staging was not transportation de luxe. "The dust is deep in summertime," ran a contemporary song, "The mountains very hard to climb;/And drivers often stop and yell,/'Get out, all hands, and push—*up hill!'* " Overnight stops were likely to mean miserable food, lumpy bunks and bedbugs. The going was rugged, however anybody tried it.

Indifferent to hardships along the way, the gold-hungry swarmed in: grizzled miners traveling light with pick, pan, and horn, young and foolish miners loaded down with blankets and grub, peddlers of sardines and tobacco, slim-fingered faro dealers, floaters without a dime, vagrants, rascals, even a few Chinese, who were promptly ejected. Stalwart fellows took the eye, like the husky young specimen described by a reporter as "a very tall, well made man, whose fine face and figure attracted our attention. . . . we ascertained that he was six feet three inches in height, and the smallest of nine brothers. He was from Iowa, weighed 180 pounds, and was only twenty-seven years old." Among hardy perennials was Major J. M. Sterling, a man well known in mining circles, highly respected for his sagacity. Having gone around the Horn in the bark *Maria* in 1820, he was now a magnificent patriarch with long white hair and splendid beard, still vigorous, still ready to assail the mountains of the high Sierras.

Some newcomers had money enough to live on for a time, some no money nor any clear notion of how to survive, much less of how to make a fortune. Others, like card sharps and stock speculators, were very sure of their profit-making methods, but they did not intend to get gold by the grubby business of digging for it.

Among incoming crowds were a corps of Teutonic damsels, cheerful and buxom, imported from Downieville to be the mainstays of the inevitable hurdy-gurdy house. No mining town was complete without a hurdy. It was a dance hall, generally small and hot, and the girls were taxi dancers who received a fixed fee per dance, often a bonus in addition when a man felt good. Miners, who frequented these places, pushed the girls around the floor to the music sawed off by one or more fiddlers or to the tinny strains of a hurdy-gurdy, and stepped on many toes with their heavy boots. A reporter unflatteringly described a hurdy girl as "the voluptuous feminine beer keg." Collectively he called them "stolid and Dutchy in expression, beery and festive in habit, with shiny foreheads and a disposition to sweat at the sound of a fiddle, as fickle as fortune and homelier than original sin."

Though they had to be sturdy, not wispy, they were not always so unattractive as all that; the imports from Downieville were said to have been good looking. For some reason, editors and others sniffed disdainfully at hurdy houses as blots on the social escutcheon, but it is hard to see why. These dance halls were boisterous and inebrious, but they were not dens of vice. They were not brothels, and the girls were not trollops. Being shoved around, bruised by flailing elbows and stepped on by stomping miners would appear to be a form of manual labor as respectable as any other kind of honest work. At any rate, disapproval notwithstanding, this new town was to have its quota of hurdies.

Besides the girls coming in, there was a small group of wives and other feminine additions. Newspaper stories imply that some of the ladies were on the rough and ready side. A startled onlooker said that when a storekeeper rebuked a female customer for unseemly language about his high prices, she doused him with a bucket of water, delivered a swift kick and pulled out a derringer with lethal intent before bystanders intervened to prevent bloodshed.

In and around Summit City a vast turmoil went on, of tree-felling, sawing and hammering as carpenters rapidly built houses, business places, and mills. Lumber was hard to come by, nearly all of it freighted in by ox teams, but a number of frame structures had gone up, the most imposing being a two-story house 32 feet by 20. A daily stage line from Gold Hill transported to within pack mule distance mining implements and provisions, which were hardly plentiful enough to keep up with the heavy demand. Toll roads were laid out all over the place: to Webber's station, sixteen miles away, and to Bowman's Ranch, eight miles, both on the Henness Pass route; to the new towns of Richport, Wightman's Camp, Lakeville.

Everywhere, said a facetious correspondent, "boiled and surged and cussed the angry crowd of gold seekers. The sight was too much for my nerves, and I inadvertently dropped seventeen drills and three picks. . . . faintly borne on the evening zephyr, came the cry, Eureka! . . . it became apparent from such exclamations as 'four bits to the pan, no boulders, work easy' . . . that surface diggings had been struck."

A. Friedman, a Virginia merchandiser, opened a store fronting the Plaza: boarding houses, restaurants and saloons—called strychnine shops—multiplied. A Hotel de Potosi appeared, also the Cosmopolitan Hotel, managed by Mrs. O'Connor of Virginia; M. C. Lake was building a commodious two-story hostelry. There were Miller and Company's book and stationery emporium, Jacob Cahn's cigar store, a real estate office run by Emmons and Cornell, of Carson City, and a brewery on the way. The town had a brass band of ten pieces, mostly from Dutch Flat, headed by William Uren, leader, and Carl York, conductor and cornet player extraordinary. "Seventy-five houses have been erected," wrote an observer in mid-August, "a hurdy-gurdy establishment is in full blast, a number of gambling houses have opened, and other indications of civilization are becoming apparent."

To report on the tremendous agitation convulsing Meadow Lake country, Virginia sent up two of its best newsmen: Dan De Quille (William Wright), of the *Territorial Enterprise,* and Alf Doten, of the *Union.* They spent about two weeks in the district, from which Doten sent ten long letters to his paper. Dan De Quille must have done equally well by the *Enterprise,* but we shall probably never know because no file of that paper is known to exist for 1865. Dan, veteran of flush times on the Comstock, crony of Mark Twain and Joe Goodman, would surely have put into his dispatches the mildly sardonic comments and genial humor that made him a popular writer in Washoe. It is regrettable that his observations on the Meadow Lake region are lost to us.

Some years later, however, he wrote a short sketch about Morris Ascheim, a Virginia barber who had no sooner landed in Summit City than he established the Sierra Nevada Shaving Saloon under a tree, digging holes in the ground to make his chair stand level. Said Dan: "We had the first shave in the new shop, and once or twice during the operation Morris threw down his razor and took up his pick . . . to regulate a leg or two of the chair. He had his combs, brushes and other tools stuck up against the trunk of the tree, and was loud in his boast of having the biggest and best-lighted barber shop in the world. . . . about a dozen other customers, who had not seen a razor in from one to six weeks, dropped in from the hills, and seated themselves upon a pine log to await their turn. The shop was a success from the start."

Ascheim was typical of enterprising young fellows who set themselves up in business in the same offhand way. A man with a sack of flour, a little salt and bacon, a fry pan, and coffee pot, might ride into town sometime during the morning. By noon he had smoothed off a log for a table and kindled a fire with the chips. Then he rang a cowbell or banged on a pan to announce the opening of a high-class restaurant. A board nailed on a tree advertised "Hon. O. Smith, Attorney at Law," the lawyer also having painted on his sign the three balls of a pawnbroker's shop. The story went that Bob Howland, of Carson City, drifting in very hungry, dined heartily at some makeshift cafe. Then, ashamed of having eaten so much, he at once went into partnership with the proprietor, contracted for lumber, and in fifteen minutes had begun to build the St. Charles Hotel, corner of Fourth and A Streets.

The Virginia reporters traveled together as a team, tramping all around the diggings, renewing acquaintance with many former inhabitants of Virginia, never refusing an invitation to step up to the bar, joking each other, sometimes sleeping under trees on a bed of tamarack boughs. "We climbed and scrambled," said Doten, "over a little the coarsest, roughest country I was ever unfortunate enough to have to pass over, it being all a rough, naked granite formation, with a few trees growing in the ravines and crevices."

At night they were often diverted and puzzled by hearing the cry of "Ho, Joe! Ho, Joe!" shouted from various parts of town, frequently from several points at the same time. Nobody named Joe ever replied. They found out that the noise was the result of a popular variety of Summit City whiskey, cheap but powerful, dispensed at one bit per glass (size of glass not stated, but probably larger than a thimble). Described as a compound of tarantula juice, Greek fire, hell's delight and tangle-leg, the stuff made a man yell that way. The more he put down the more wildly he shouted "Ho, Joe!"

Doten remarked that the whiskey was a brand that "cannot be mistaken either in smell, taste or its effects. Why, the very first drink of it makes a man's finger ends tingle and the roots of his hair pull . . . and he shouts 'Ho, Joe!' at once. A second drink makes him see stars. The third . . . will make him forget to pay for his liquor. At the fourth . . . he commences to tell lies about his best friend. The fifth drink completely demoralizes him; he

does not recognize his creditors when he sees them . . . and finds
it impossible to tell the truth." Dan, he went on, after solemnly
promising to drink nothing stronger than wine on this trip, suc-
cumbed within an hour, then wrote his *Enterprise* letters under
the spell of the fourth and fifth drinks of Ho Joe.

The words, Doten said, originated in Nevada City, where the
wife of a venerable miner named Joe was always fearful that the
old gentleman, weaving home after a night on the town with
friends, would break his neck by tumbling into an open mine
shaft. Whenever he did not show up at the usual unseemly hour,
she would tour the diggings, calling into every shaft, "Ho, Joe!
Ho, Joe!" Apparently Joe never fell in, but she made the rounds
so often that miners in the neighborhood took up the cry and
brought it with them to Meadow Lake, where it became a sort
of slogan or nickname for the district. One man up there called
his claim Ho Joe, and another suggested that the next new town
be named Ho Joe City.

Although the Virginia newsmen enjoyed the sociability they
met along the way, they did not neglect the main part of their
duty, which was to report on the mining resources of the region.
Doten faithfully recorded a monotonous quantity of prosy facts:
The New York Company is developing a ledge with very good
prospects. . . . The Parker shows a fine six feet ledge. . . . The
Indian Boy Company have a shaft some twelve feet in depth. . . .
The Summit Ruby is 900 feet in length. . . . and so forth and so
on about dozens of ledges, claims, and companies.

That sort of dull stuff, he said, was "a confoundedly musty
subject to some people; it is to me," but gold country papers
printed it by the yard. Columns of statistics on the number of feet
owned by various companies, length of tunnels, depth of shafts,
learned descriptions impressively bristling with scientific terms
geological and chemical, data on stamp mills, hoisting machinery,
force pumps, and the like: this information was eagerly read by
miners, especially by those whose claims had been written up,
and accepted as gospel, too. The mining pundit of the time de-

livered his pronouncements with an air of assurance much like that of the political and social pundit of today.

Imaginative reporters, bored by the commonplaces of mining news, parodied these humdrum accounts. "I am confident," said one humorist, "that ledges holding in solution considerable feldspar, mica, hornblende, tule, turpentine, carbonate of lime, sulphate of lime, chloride of sodium, iron pyrites and coal oil, will for a long time remain undeveloped . . . in this district." A joker solemnly discussed the Rumbuzzle mine, the Folderol, Tooiallooial and others. On the Bamboozle, he said,

The vein rock is strongly carbonized, fossilized and dramatized; character of the hanging wall, oxygenic, hydrocenic, nitrogenic and hygienic; that of the foot wall, talcose, quartose, squirtose, and verbose . . . the country rock is not only lymphatic, cathartic and diuretic, but also paregoric, parabolic and rheumatic. . . . The Skedaddle is a splendid looking vein, and I have no doubt that by it a large fortune will soon be taken from the pockets of its owner. The gossan . . . overlaps the flucan for several miles, a sure indication that there is something in the vein. . . . The proprietors are bound to "strike it" at the depth of 1800 or 1900 feet.

An anonymous wit invented a location notice: "Know all men (or one woman, for then all will know) that the undersigned, who is an individual of limited means, but of unlimited expectations, locates, claims, and intends to hold and work two claims of two hundred feet each on this ledge, containing, as he believes and hopes it does, gold, silver, calespar, feldspar, and spar the bar-keep, besides other precious metals, too numerous to mention, together with all dips, spurs, and angles and triangles ranging from vertical to horizontal. . . . To be known as the Elephant Ledge and Company." Professor Noncommittal, after inspecting the Big Goosetherumfoodle mine, submitted a report:

There is undoubtedly a mine here if the ore bodies hold out. The gangue rock is favorable to the existence of ore, and the overlapping seams of schistose show an undoubted tendency to productiveness in rock, which may be ore bearing. While I refrain from pronouncing with certainty on the Big Goosetherumfoodle mine, still I argue that as great expectations regarding the yield of this vein may be maintained as of any other ground in this vicinity. . . . I would advise the

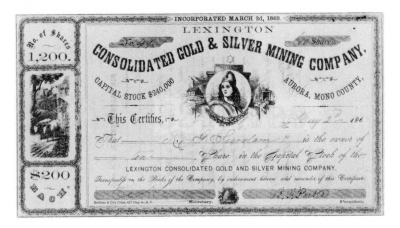

A mining stock certificate—not of a Meadow Lake company, but probably representative.

*Bancroft Library, University of California, Berkeley.*

sinking of 100 shafts ten feet apart through the hardest rock which can be found. . . . If the rock prove rich the mine will be valuable. If the rock prove very rich the mine will then prove very valuable. It should be borne in mind that if it is necessary to sink deep on the vein the lode must be penetrated further than if not.

Doten, hewing to the factual line, praised the Enterprise ledge of 1,500 feet, and he had hopeful words for a few others, but in general he, too, was noncommittal. On most of the claims he found that little work had been done, only enough labor to hold the ground in accordance with the mining laws of the district: shallow openings in the croppings, hardly a single shaft down as far as twenty feet. He was dubious about the difficulty of working the hard granite, and about the high cost of getting out the rock. He also questioned the wisdom of founding a city

before the mines had proved that they could support its hoped-
for population of some ten thousand people. Whether "this noted
district," he concluded, "is . . . the richest on the Pacific coast or
the biggest 'bilk,' I don't really know . . . neither does anyone
else."

Around Meadow Lake, any attitude other than whole-
hearted confidence did not get much of a hearing. Doten's re-
straint was a minority report, overborne by splendid stories that
bombarded the press of California and Nevada. Ecstatic accounts sent in by men on the scene had an authoritative tone that
made skepticism difficult. Said one paper: "We do not hesitate
in saying that this district is destined at no distant day to become
the most famous for wealth yet discovered on this coast or anywhere else." Another spoke of "croppings from the California
claim, in which free gold was to be seen as large as peas." An
exuberant correspondent exclaimed: "I have seen it all, and
without any hesitation I pronounce it the richest and most extensive mining district I have ever seen."

Such positive statements, made by experienced men who
were supposed to know the difference between a quartz ledge
and a wildcat, carried weight. Doten himself remarked upon the
frenzied optimism of Summit City. "All day," he said, "the noise
of the hammer and saw mingles with the booming of blasts, and
people are passing hither and thither excitedly in all directions,
there being constant rumors coming in of rich strikes and new
discoveries all around."

Excitement became delirium when some wag induced a
credulous man to wash dirt from within town limits, then slyly
salted a panful with a little gold dust. News of this good "prospect" set off a terrific uproar as the gold-hungry tumbled over
each other in a riotous stampede. Within an hour the entire town
site was staked off for placer diggings, hysterical locaters tack-
ing notices on houses: "This lot is claimed for mining purposes
by so-and-so." One indignant storekeeper loudly complained:
"By Shesuskrist, I pays four hundred dollar for mine lot no

more as two weeks ago, and now, py Got, dey takes it from me!"
But before the town could be rooted up, the joker explained the
hoax, claim notices came down, and lot holders relaxed.

Another sort of excitement occurred when about twenty
citizens jumped the Plaza, fenced it off and camped there determined to hold it. No self-respecting mining community could
tolerate jumping of property, whether public or private. A town
meeting directed an attorney to draw up a remonstrance against
the jumpers and to give them one hour to vacate. In an orderly
manner a citizens' committee, accompanied by 250 townsmen,
marched up to the Plaza to serve the remonstrance. The jumpers
considered it, then swore they would hold the premises anyhow, and threatened to shoot anybody who touched the fence.
Their belligerence ended peaceful negotiations. Irate townsmen
tore the fence apart, and there was a brief scrimmage, Sheriff
Brokaw clouting with telling effect. Nervous gun-toters fired
random shots, one of which slightly wounded a man, but the
only other casualties were a few black eyes and bloody noses as
the jumpers were forcibly dislodged.

The victors immediately reared a flagpole in the middle of
the Plaza, then gave three rousing cheers as they ran up the
colors. John Lambert, a leader of the jumpers and one of the
gun-brandishers, was brought to trial by the Justice of the Peace,
who fined him $100. When Lambert said he was unable to pay,
the judge discharged him on condition that he pay the fine sometime. In an interesting comment on the ways of mining towns,
a correspondent said that "the people of this place *expect him
to do it.*"

By late summer, 1865, gold fever yet raged at the same
high temperature. Nearly every day, said one story, "there is
brought to town rock that is literally covered with the precious
metal; and every locater that we have conversed with, is just
on the point of being a rich man. . . . The rush still continues;
prospectors in every direction . . . packing ore on mules and in
their pockets." They staked off ground at the rate of a mile a day.

On file in the office of the Nevada County Recorder were 741 company locations and 10,910 individual claims of 100 feet each, for a total of 1,091,000 feet.

When lumber was available, buildings went up remarkably fast. "The open lot of yesterday," said a letter-writer, "receives the skeleton of a two-story building, to be by tomorrow clothed and inhabited by its excited and wealthy (?) owner." Summit City had ten stores, five lumber yards, ten hotels, five blacksmith shops, four hurdy-gurdies, and numerous bars—100, according to one reckoning, but somebody may have been too befuddled to count. The brewery of Fitzmire & Flurshutz was a going concern. More business houses than any other town in the county except Nevada City and Grass Valley produced a hubbub like that of Montgomery Street in San Francisco.

The price of lots soared to $800. Mining stocks changed hands at 50¢ to $150 a foot. The Pacific Company turned down a San Francisco offer of $16,000 for 800 feet. The Enterprise Company received a bid of $100,000 for a quarter interest in that ledge but apparently did not sell. Among transitory residents was said to be an occasional New York capitalist attracted by the lure of profitable investments. His real or fancied presence led to talk that New York companies intended to put up quartz mills the following spring.

The goose was hanging high in a region that seemed blessed by great prosperity. Summit City was easily the leading town in the district, but rival towns, besides Richport, Baltimore City, and Lakeville, had sprouted like grass in spring rain—all of them, in the minds of their creators, destined for a future permanent and profitable. Across Meadow Lake was Hudsonville, composed of two sawmills. A mile away was Excelsior, near the mine of that name. Mendoza, on Bloody Run near the Enterprise ledge, appeared to be thriving. Atlanta, in Fordyce valley, had two frame buildings and one resident, Jerome Fordyce. At the base of Old Man Mountain was a town site without a house and without a name.

Within a year, said a confident correspondent, every one of those places would be "filled with a population pursuing the mechanic arts or delving into the bowels of the earth for the rich ore that is even now sparkling on its surface." There was some doubt about the survival of Atlanta. A proposed dam across the outlet of the lake there would flood the valley, but Fordyce said that he did not intend to be drowned out by a dam site.

A great hum of noisy industry conveyed an impression of an economy flushed with health and vigor. The impression was delusive. Expansive hopes of wealth were still no more than hopes, something promised but not yet bestowed. Affluence had stalled by the wayside. The Meadow Lake district looked like the big thing, sure enough, the biggest ever—almost everybody seemed convinced of that—yet somehow it had perversely withheld lavish rewards.

Details on actual cash returns from claims were meager and far from arresting. Miners who panned croppings took up to $10 a day. Men working the Wisconsin claim with an arrastre—Americanized to "raster"—a primitive device for crushing ores by dragging around in a circular bed a heavy stone attached to a sweep, made about $25 a day each. On the Mohawk, working decomposed surface quartz with a rocker yielded $24 a day per man. Such incomes were not to be sneered at, but they were hardly commensurate with assays of staggering size. The Enterprise Company was selling second-class ore at $40 a ton. That was not big money either. Gamblers and barkeepers were raking in profits, as usual, and perhaps a few merchants, but no stream of gold was pouring into miners' pockets.

All summer the news implied that five or six Meadow Lake quartz mills would be ready to go day after tomorrow. It was not so. Mill buildings were going up, and machinery was lying around at various sites, but it was in no condition to function. By late September the California mill was supposed to be in running order "in three or four weeks." The Enterprise

mill might have got under way had not somebody neglected to
ship amalgamator pin castings from San Francisco. When experts concluded that Meadow Lake ore had to be treated with
hot water, getting boilers from Oakland or somewhere meant
more delay. Only the mill of Winton and Robinson was fitfully
operating.

Rock for crushing had to be transported by pack mule or ox
teams forty or sixty miles to mills at Virginia, Nevada City or
Grass Valley in driblets of half a ton or less up to five-ten tons
or so at a time. It was a long haul, expensive, laborious and slow;
an ox team took days and days to get anywhere. So far only
small amounts of ore had been milled, sometimes merely a few
hundred pounds of surface rock on an experimental basis. Yields
ran from less than $30 per ton to over three hundred, none of
the figures coming close to those large assays. Data on crushing
did not always get into the news, or were given vaguely as
"good results"—as if they were actually too disappointing to
publish. To anybody who read between the lines, it was clear
that the supposedly rich ledges were not giving up spectacular
quantities of gold.

So the apparent economic soundness of the district was
illusory. The place hummed with a great deal of action, a great
deal of determined hustling around, some of it aimless, much
of it involved with construction, freighting in supplies and machinery, making roads, sawing lumber, digging wells, digging
mine shafts, blasting. All that was called dead-work: i.e., work
not directly productive of returns but necessary for future ex-
ploitation. Any mining district generally required a certain
amount of dead-work; this untamed Sierra Nevada country
called for a prodigious expenditure of grueling labor merely to
prepare for the business of extracting gold. Dead-work in this
region overloaded the debit side of the ledger.

Most mine owners had done no more than barely scratch
the surface of their claims. Not surprising perhaps, considering
the unyielding granite of those mountains. Like iron, one man
said. He swore he had seen a drill-hole fifteen inches deep that

"positively required the drills to be sharpened *forty-six* times
to penetrate to that depth." Possibly he was stretching the truth,
but the hardness was a fact. It bothered even the larger companies, which had trouble breaking through adamantine walls;
it was stubborn enough to cool the ardor of the most impetuous
treasure-seeker.

Meadow Lakers found out what quartz hunters always
learned: that hard rock mining was the most complicated and
costly of all methods. Gold might be tantalizingly visible in
quartz, but getting it out was not as simple as panning gravel.
A vein needed substantial capital for development. In these
diggings the expenditure of a few hundred dollars on a claim
made hardly a dent. Milling machinery, hoisting machinery,
equipment for blasting, tools for tunneling and the like: these
necessaries meant plenty of money that the Meadow Lake boys,
by and large, did not have. Their best hope lay in demonstrat-
ing that their claims were good, then selling out for a good
price. But they could not get far enough into the granite to
prove much of anything, and moneyed men had become cau-
tious about taking chances on undeveloped ground that looked
like wildcat.

Unfavorable portents shadowed extravagant assertions of
rich discoveries and grandiose expectations of wealth. Whatever
the auguries, however, the people of Summit City seemed unaware of any cloud on the horizon. They behaved as if there
were no such word as fail. Every rock sharp gloated over a
pocketful of specimens crusted with the precious yellow metal,
and astonishing news was common—as when a blast on the Enterprise ledge threw out two and a half tons of ore described as
"perfectly lousy with gold."

Until early autumn the town careened along with undimin-
ished velocity in an atmosphere festive and sociable. It was as
gay as a carnival where light-hearted folks ride the merry-go-
round without a care in the world. In that stimulating climate
abounded the good health that encourages the jocund temper.
The place was not a haven for cantankerous gaffers or irritable

dyspeptics, and nobody died—not yet anyhow. Town fathers had not even thought of setting aside a plot for a graveyard. "There is a chance now, however, for a commencement," said Alf Doten, "for two druggists, two doctors and a priest arrived in town the day before we left."

By day miners dispersed through the mountains to put in a blast or two on their claims or, better still, to ramble around prospecting for richer ones and loading themselves down with yet more rock samples. Toward evening back they came to congregate around huge bonfires, where they swapped yarns about good strikes and built castles in the air. As daytime absentees trooped in, the night became uproarious with hurdy music, the house-shaking stamping of dancing feet, the whooping of miners whirling girls around the floor, snarling dog fights, now and then a screeching woman fight, howls of "Ho, Jo!" The racket, together with the movement of dusky figures flitting about in firelight, "bring to my mind," a correspondent said, "Dante's picture of hell." By midnight the hullabaloo generally subsided, to be followed some hours later by the incessant ringing of breakfast bells.

Raucousness made carping visitors believe that Summit City was uncivilized. "Society in this place," said a reporter, "is decidedly in a crude, wild state, nothing in that respect being regulated properly as yet." One critic opined that what the place needed was a zealous missionary accustomed to dealing with heathen tribes.

Nevertheless, if the town did not merit a good-conduct medal or a citation for godliness—not a single Bible on the premises, one shocked letter-writer observed—neither was it scandalously sinful. It was more law-abiding than might have been expected. The boys got drunk and noisy as they were bound to do, and collided in fist fights as they were also bound to do; they frittered away too much time and money in gambling joints; some of them (not many) jumped claims; they possessed about the usual assortment of human weaknesses and follies. But there was no crime wave here, no outbreaks of thievery, no rape or murder, no red light sisterhood, no drink-crazed loons shooting up each other and the town. If young men got saturated with cheap whiskey, then released their exuberance by yelling and punching each other, that was better than mayhem.

On fine moonlight nights, when the band played old favorite melodies from an antiquated scow out on the lake, idyllic peace momentarily supplanted tumult. Pastimes were not limited to hurdy-gurdy, barroom, and monte table. Miners put on a minstrel show in the quarters of the new Bank Exchange saloon, assisted by an orchestra of piano, violin, and Carl York's cornet. A violin solo, by Professor John Hardin, was received with loud applause. The whole affair, said a reporter, "by aid of burnt cork . . . two gallons of Ho Joe whiskey and a great deal of minstrel talent, was a decided success."

M. C. Lake celebrated the completion of his fine hotel, the Lake House, by giving a ball on the roomy second floor. Only thirteen ladies were present, but they made up for their lack of numbers by good looks and dancing skill; they and the gentlemen footed it in a sprightly way to the music of two violins and a cello. "The genial countenance of the host," an observer remarked, "together with the smiles of his estimable lady, shed a sunshine of joy and welcome over the happy scene."

Somewhat more elaborate was Mrs. Smith's Farewell Ball, an elegant occasion managed by a Committee on Carriages (probably nobody had a carriage up there at the summit), a Reception Committee, and a Committee on Supply. Tickets read: "Calico Dresses and Gray Shirts admitted; tickets one dollar fifty." Some joker wrote that when the dancers were ready for the midnight collation, Mrs. Smith rushed in to say that the Committee on Supply (Billy Allen and Charley Parker) had stolen all the tea and sandwiches. We found, "to our utter astonishment and disgust," said this writer, "that Parker and Allen had pledged the entire supper to the landlady of the St. Charles for their week's board."

Bob Howland, popular manager of the St. Charles, often figured in joshing stories. One was that, soon after he opened his hotel, a number of his old friends flocked in, threw their traps into a corner and called out, "Hello, Bob! you infernal old thief! If I ain't glad to see you may I be d—d!" Then they made themselves at home, "never missing a meal and never paying a cent. The butcher finally shut down on meat . . . the milkman shut down on milk and the baker on bread. Bob explained the matter to his lodgers, who, to a man, swore they would not desert him. They would whip the butcher, the milkman, the baker, or any other man Bob wanted whipped, and if no more meat, milk or bread could be had, they would worry along on boiled cabbage and potatoes, or any other cheap stuff."

Besides dancing, inhabitants enjoyed other entertainments. A performer who called himself Mons. De Lay pleased a crowd of several hundred with a tight wire act on a cable stretched from a stump to a pine tree. He did his stunts like a Blondin, walking up and down, sitting on the cable, standing on one foot, all without losing his balance. Spectators applauded with cheerful good will, but when the hat went around they did not chip in liberally, to the great, but unspoken, disgust of Mons. De Lay.

Additional innocuous diversions suggest a tranquil village: raffles and soirees, foot races, picnics, by early autumn an occasional church service. To somebody from a staid eastern community, this town in the mountains might have seemed uncouth, but, though not truly urban or sophisticated, it was not very wild and woolly either. Certainly it did not look disreputable. Composed of brand new buildings, most of them freshly painted, it had a spruce appearance, bright and shining.

As in all other mining towns, Summit City people relished anything that looked like a celebration. So with hilarious enthusiasm they welcomed a distinguished visitor: James W. Nye, United States Senator from Nevada and former Governor of that state. The citizenry turned out en masse, the band sounded off with vigor, cannon boomed, everybody hurrahed. From a stand in front of the St. Charles Hotel, the senator made a long speech. Introduced by the Hon. N. W. Winton, State Senator from Storey County, Nevada, Nye spoke for an hour and a half —though correspondents neglected to say what he talked about. After that loud cheers and more shooting. B. F. Whittemore, proprietor of the Excelsior Hotel, and Edwin Fowler, a notary public, entertained Senator Nye and others at the Bank Exchange, the party graced by some twenty ladies. Ho Joe whiskey flowed freely all day, of course, for the rank and file, but for the senator probably something better: perhaps Otard brandy or Old Bourbon or Green Seal champagne. The Bank Exchange and other Summit City bars stocked the best of bottled goods for those who had the price.

In late September the first snow forecast the coming of winter. A few weeks afterward, winds of gale force, roaring through at night, blew down two buildings and shook the town like an earthquake. The populace was so alarmed that nobody dared to sleep. Then a hard rain turned to driving snow that soon piled up to a foot and a half.

By this time immigration had practically ceased. For some weeks the flow had been reversing itself as a good many residents departed for warmer climes in valleys below, most of them intending to return to the mountains in the spring. Summit City merchants had been stocking up on groceries and other supplies to see them through snowbound months; some 200 townspeople, including about forty women and a bevy of children, elected to spend the winter in the high Sierras. The exodus made the town look rather deserted, but it was not dead, only going into hibernation to dream of a brilliant awakening when the snow was gone. The hopeful ones clung to the belief that the future was sure to be good. A correspondent said: "We have seen half a dozen mining towns built upon the mountains, including the city of Virginia, and we shall be disappointed if Summit City does not eclipse them all next year in the rapidity of its growth."

# 4

XXXXXXXXXXXX

# Sierra Winter 1865-66

WINTER moved in with a businesslike no-nonsense air about it, not boisterously, but steadily insistent. Three feet of snow became five feet, then seven, then ten. Summit City residents took to watching the Plaza flagpole as a measuring stick while the fall piled up. As one reporter put it: "on the very summit of the Sierras in Winter . . . the keenest vision in the clearest weather fails to penetrate beyond her broad belt of snow." For a while no violent storms raged among the crags, so that the onset of the season, as winters went in these parts, was not unduly severe.

As the town settled into cold-weather rhythm, business decelerated, became dull, and most of the hotels closed their doors. Only the Lake House and the Excelsior kept open house, not that they expected crowds of transient lodgers, but mainly to serve as oases for the sociably inclined. Very few people arrived or left, but whoever wanted to get in or out could do so if he had enough determination. Roads were too deeply drifted for travel, yet the place was not completely cut off from the rest of the world. Several times a week a pack and saddle train floundered through to Polley's station on the Dutch Flat road, taking two days for the ten-mile trip. The most reliable means of communication was a superb ski artist named Granville "Zack"

Zachariah, of Downieville. His one-man company, Zack's Snow-shoe Express, sped over the mountains on periodic trips carrying some 60 pounds of mail, papers, sometimes ore samples, anything not too bulky to impede his skimming progress.

Zack became an institution. One writer called him "our snow shoe heeled Mercury. . . . he is a stunner; a velocipede; he comes up over the crest of the Enterprise ridge, with the regularity of astral movement, and before I can wink he scoots down into Bloody Run, leaving a trail of feathery snow flakes in his wake like the tail of a comet." Another admirer said: "What Peter, the Hermit, was to the Crusaders, what My Man Friday was to Robinson Crusoe, so is Zack to the worthy inhabitants of Summit City and its 'surroundings.' Rain, hail or snow, sunshine or clouds, the Express must be brought through." People up there got their letters off, and faithful correspondents kept in touch with editors below.

Zack's speed and swooping skill were an inspiration. Just about everybody in town tried the newfangled Norwegian snowshoes. Generally homemade, they were no doubt clumsy enough to make a specialist from St. Moritz turn up his nose, but they worked. Men, women, and children took headers into snowbanks, sprawled awkwardly and suffered involuntary down-sittings on the hard-packed surface while they learned how to ski without falling. Henry Hartley, himself an expert, should have been a competent teacher; perhaps he showed novices how to stay on their feet, part of the time anyhow. The athletic ones caught on fast.

On clear days they raced down slopes and kept it up after the moon rose, making the frosty air ring with whoop and halloo. If they did not know a slalom from an immelman turn, they knew how to get over the ground on skis and how to get to the top of a slope without benefit of ski lift. They became strongly opinionated, too, about the proper kind of "dope" to smear on the underside of runners to prevent snow from sticking. Usually having a base of axle grease, dope was compounded according to numerous formulas by numerous authorities, each claiming that his brand was the best, each stimulating heated arguments.

Among star performers was the feminine contingent. Many of the ladies, a reporter said, "have become experts on the snow-shoe, and compete favorably in the steeplerace with their com-peers of the hardy sex. They climb to the top of the surrounding hills, and with the speed of a falcon sweeping down upon its prey, they dash by the crowd of spectators with pole balanced in mid-air and all colors set." The snowshoe became such a familiar means of getting around that four couples took off for a dance at Webber's station, ten miles away, leaving Summit City at four in the afternoon, arriving in plenty of time for a lively evening, then skiing home again.

A popular sport was double skiing, the lady standing on the runners behind the gentleman and holding on to him. A man from Dutch Flat, who tried that, told of his sad experience. His partner, he said, was "a prepossessing damsel on the shady side of forty, with corkscrew curls of beautiful pink hue, vege-table countenance and calico eye-brows," whom he called Biddy O'Who. "With mingled hope, fear and a straight whiskey that limbered us up like a boiled macaroni," he went on, he launched himself and rider from the crest. All went well for a time, but then , alas, "We experience a sensation of falling. We clutch the empty air, gasp for breath, shut our eyes and over we go. (Earth-quakes of applause by the natives that made the welkin ring for miles around.) . . . Biddy was a total wreck. . . . waterfall, rats, teeth, wigs, gutta percha calves and unmentionables innum-erable . . . were strewn around in the wildest confusion, and on all sides met our distorted gaze."

Summit City was something like a ski resort almost a hun-dred years before the winter Olympics at Squaw Valley in the neighborhood of Lake Tahoe not far away. One difference was that reporters then, unlike their modern counterparts, did not dilate at length on Meadow Lake sports togs, especially for women. What the girls wore would be interesting to know, but we are not told what was fashionable for ski runs. The voluminous skirts of the day seem an unwieldy costume for fast maneuvering, but if they were supplanted by a more efficient outfit, writers failed to mention it. A reasonable guess is that the ladies did not appear in stretch pants.

The frank on an unused envelope. Possibly this is the frank of the famous Snowshoe Thomson.

*Wells Fargo Bank, History Room, San Francisco.*

Now and then hurricane winds, blizzards that buried the Plaza flagpole, and temperamental rainstorms put snowshoers out of action, but until early April they were out there on the slopes whenever the surface was right. Yet resourceful Summit City people, when not chopping wood and keeping stoves well stoked, also enjoyed indoor pastimes entertaining and cultural. These homely doings, much like those of any other small town in the 19th century, contrast refreshingly with machine-made diversions of today.

A dancing academy, directed by Professor Snyder, gave its pupils plenty of practice in frequent dances at the Bank Exchange, having no difficulty in rounding up a quorum of feminine partners. For these occasions the saloon proprietors obligingly cleared the floor and, in deference to the ladies, closed their bar.

Small fry attended a school, which was supported by private contributions. The teacher, a Mr. Van Cleve, introduced the mysteries of grammar and arithmetic to sixteen young scholars. The drama appealed strongly, as it always had in mining towns since the days of '49. Amateur thespians, who staged plays every week, aided the school by benefit performances of "The Two Bonnycastles," "The Spirit Table" and others. An industrious man named Denton was building a theater at Bloody Run, rounding up artisans and sending axemen out in midwinter to fell timber.

Young men organized a literary and debating society that circulated a manuscript newspaper. Thomas Hannah, President *pro tem,* delivered a spirited inaugural address in which, said the Gold Hill *News,* he "calls upon the . . . News to assist them in procuring a wet nurse for one of the old bachelors out there." Those so-called old bachelors, probably all aged 35 to 40 or thereabouts, gave themselves a dinner, excluding the younger set.

Thoughtful townsmen took to dropping in at the Lake House for informal discussions philosophical and scientific. On almost any evening, said a letter-writer, a listener "would think he was in the presence of *savans* and *literati,* and not in the company of honest miners and wood choppers. Vulgar bricks and mortar they wholly ignore, and are only intent on primary and secondary geological formations." No doubt they also discussed political issues and the character of President Johnson, who was feuding with Congress and making newspapers sound off in fuming editorials.

When the literary society disintegrated because of dissatisfaction over debate decisions, it was succeeded by the Nasty Club, which conducted mock trials of members on trumped-up charges. One man was arraigned for malpractice in felling a tree. A witness for the prosecution testified that the tree looked as if it had been chewed down by beavers; another deposed that it appeared to have been struck by lightning. The jury found defendant guilty, and the judge fined him a round of drinks for the club. The culprit, like a gentleman, promptly paid his fine.

Real litigation in the court of Judge J. E. Jones attracted interested audiences. The first case was brought by the schoolteacher, Van Cleve, for non-payment of tuition against a man with a large family. The jury brought in a verdict for the plaintiff, and assessed the defendent for $57.50. Whereupon Friedman, the affable merchandiser, invited all jurymen to his establishment, the Magnolia Billiard Saloon, where he uncorked several bottles of Heidsieck. Judge Jones continued to hear a number of petty cases, but none was a mining lawsuit. There were no long wrangles over disputed claim ownerships, no manipulation of mining legalisms of the sort that gladdened the hearts and fattened the wallets of lawyers in a town like Virginia.

Apropos of lawyers, an attorney who arrived in Summit City to hang out his shingle in late winter was Orion Clemens, former Secretary of State of Nevada Territory, and brother of Mark Twain. When Tod Robinson sued Whittemore, proprietor of the Excelsior Hotel, to recover $8.75 for services, Clemens appeared for the defendant, plaintiff conducting his own case. "The learned ex-public functionary," said a spectator, "was too much for poor Tod, and the jury brought in a verdict for defendants." Mark Twain, who was often exasperated by the idiosyncrasies of his elder brother, acknowledged that Orion was a capable lawyer.

A furore arose over selection of representatives to an important miners' convention in Sacramento. To choose somebody, there was, of course, the traditional public meeting. It picked several delegates—Brumsey, Hannah, Thomas Cox, and others —but somehow that decision was ignored, another meeting occurred, then another and still another. Every night, said a correspondent, "we have a meeting—six meet together in solemn conclave and swear that their appointees are the men most suitable to attend the Miners' Convention. . . . another night, more than six assemble together, and in their majesty of might annul the proceedings of the previous evening, and so on ad infinitum." These councils, reverberant with what one irritated writer called "the usual number of resolutions and whereases, and a countless number of buncombe speeches," failed to agree on anybody.

Thus, to the great disgust of up-and-coming citizens, this highly-praised gold region sent no representative to the convention. It was lamentable, said one, that all the palaver had not succeeded in dispatching "one of the sovereigns to Sacramento to represent this truly auriferous district." Nevertheless, the meeting-goers had had a good time expressing themselves. Miners relished meetings, they liked to talk, and they were averse to conducting business in a hurry. Public gatherings were generally long-winded.

In such ways the people of the high Sierras found winter months no great hardship. They invented their own methods, serious and frivolous, for making life interesting, and they were not bored. They petitioned the California Company, owners of the town site, to designate suitable space for burial grounds to be called the Excelsior Necropolis. This petition coincided with a distressing shortage of whiskey, but everybody hoped that by the time the plea was granted, enough Ho Joe would have been sledded in to celebrate with eclat.

Pranksters played practical jokes and staged sham duels. Nobody having much money, men traded mining stocks by a system of barter, and that, too, was a game. One waggish correspondent said that everybody was broke except one lucky fellow, who "is watched from the rising of the sun to the going down thereof; and if he is seen carrying a ham or a quart of cranberries, the word is given, a 'surprise party' is gotten up, and he is cleaned out in no time." Minor incidents were amusing— like the man giving an impassioned temperance lecture in the Bank Exchange and pausing off and on for a hearty swig from a suspicious looking black bottle.

Not at all amusing, however, was a fire in late winter. Fire was the scourge of all western communities. It was a dreaded menace that, once off to a good start on a windy day, swept through those wooden towns with fury uncontrollable. Fire had ravaged San Francisco, Nevada City, Grass Valley, and Virginia. This one, breaking out in the Excelsior bakery, might have destroyed the whole place but for the prompt action of many volunteer firemen. While some ripped shingles from the roof, others subdued the blaze with a barrage of snowballs.

Winter, that covered ledges with drifts, was not a good time for prospecting, and gold-hunters stayed home. Yet the mining front was not moribund. N. W. Winton contracted in San Francisco for a steam engine and boiler for a mill to be built by the owners of the Indian Boy ledge. They had got out about a hundred tons of rock described as "first-class ore." The California mill celebrated Christmas Day by making its first cleanup, the rock yielding $69 to the ton. The owners of a hitherto unsung claim called Gold Cabin agreed to deliver somewhere 1,000 tons of surface rock of guaranteed high quality. The Enterprise Company was reported to be "taking out an immense quantity of rich rock"; as they delved deeper into the vein, every blast disclosed "richer ore than above." James Battersby, secretary of that company, displayed specimens that assayed $800 to the ton. Fifty feet of the Enterprise ledge were said to have been sold in San Francisco for $300 a foot.

In Virginia, trading in mining stocks was brisk, Meadow Lake shares selling at $50 to $250 a foot. A San Francisco gentleman in Virginia innocently inquired whether the district up there at the summit was as important as all the handsome stories made it out to be. An astonished *Enterprise* reporter "took this doubting Thomas to see a large collection of selected rock from that locality which would assay from $250 to $50,000 to the ton."

Mining news had a familiar ring that comforted and reassured. It cheered Summit City inhabitants, and reminded them, if they needed a reminder, of their chief reason for being where they were. One or two disturbing accounts mentioned a peculiarity of the gold in Meadow Lake ledges: somewhere below the surface it joined up with other metals, mainly with iron in combinations called sulphurets, and would not let go. The result was a large loss of virgin gold. The loss might be prevented, some believed, by use of this or that "process," but nobody was sure about it. This talk was unsettling, but offsetting it were confident reports on fine surface rock and stunning assays.

When the spring of 1866 seemed not far away, at least on the calendar if not on the snow-covered earth, forward-looking men envisaged good times ahead. A Mr. Calder asked the state assembly for a franchise to lay water pipes in the streets of the town. Wells Fargo sent up a man from Auburn to open an express office in the high Sierras. The Federal government authorized a postoffice and appointed a postmaster, but he had not appeared. To give the town proper status, a few prominent citizens drew up a petition to Nevada County representatives in the California legislature, praying that legislation incorporate Summit City. This petition they conceived and forwarded on their own responsibility without having canvassed the views of their fellow townsmen.

The gesture was well-meaning but misguided. It stirred up a great rumpus among people who were affronted at being bypassed in this high-handed manner. Between them and others who were inclined to approve the action of the petitioners arose the sharp difference of opinion that was typical of a place like this one. "Mountain towns," said a correspondent, "will have their splits whether they boast two churches, one, or as in this instance, none. Why, sir, I have known one-half of the sovereigns of a mountain village ready to cut the other half's throats over the respective merits of the different styled sewing machines—if nothing else presented."

In this conflict, indignant objectors were more vocal than their easy-going opponents. The disgruntled faction called a meeting to protest, not against the petition itself, but against the secret way of framing it and sending it off. This meeting was the most incoherent of all the mixed-up meetings of the season.

Called to order at 7 P.M. by a Mr. Morton, the assembly grappled with the first item of business, election of a chairman. Several gentlemen simultaneously nominated half a dozen men, but all except two declined to be considered. The struggle to choose one of the pair became so warm and chaotic that a variety of votes were taken: a voice vote, then a vote by show of hands, then by division to right and left, then by ballot. Concurrent with these maneuvers and interrupting them was a steady stream of suggestion and argument. After about an hour or more, Mr. Andrews, proprietor of the Andrews Hotel, was elected to chair the session.

Not being an experienced parliamentarian, he was too inept to keep matters under control. In short order they were threshing around in a bog of motions, counter-motions, and objections. When somebody made a motion, somebody else offered an amendment, and four or five jumped up to debate it hotly, all speaking at once. Then a fellow who had proposed neither motion nor amendment would shout, "I accept that amendment." Sometimes the motion was voted on before the amendment, sometimes after, and the chairman generally forgot to call for negative votes. The noisy disorder, in a rich mixture of Irish brogue, miner's English, broken German and Scandinavian, led one spectator to remark: "I can compare the proceedings to nothing else than the confusion that reigned at the Tower of Babel."

Still, the assembly did evolve some sort of remonstrance against the sub rosa incorporation petition. About midnight it was proposed that a collection be taken up to defray the expenses of Sheriff Brokaw in conveying this document to the Nevada County delegation. But when the hat started around, most of the protestors headed for the door, thus adjourning the meeting. Yet oddly enough, when they met again the next evening, discussions were orderly and productive. This gathering appointed a committee to draft provisions to be submitted to the state legislature for the incorporation of the town.

The committee drew up an elaborate bill that called for a mayor, for aldermen and all other officers proper to a large community. It also asked that the name of the town be changed to Meadow Lake, chiefly because of another Summit City in Alpine County. For some time people there had been grumbling about mixups over mail sent to the wrong place. They maintained that they had a better right to the name because their town was two years older and was at a higher altitude, too. The altitude claim was warmly refuted, but Nevada County petitioners, recognizing the confusion inherent in identical names, prayed that their town be called Meadow Lake.

By the middle of April work gangs were digging out some of the nearby roads. It was a minor effort that did not clear the way for rapid transit, but such news had a good sound. Zack had given up his snowshoes in favor of express by saddle horse. Travelers could come in from Heaton's station by mule train, which usually left there at 2 A.M. to take advantage of the crust of snow, and arrived in Summit City about noon.

Optimism was in the air. One writer estimated that the population of Summit City "will be 10,000 before the first of August; most of the people set it even higher yet." When the snow disappeared, said another, the town "will rise to sudden greatness and renown more rapidly than the Virginia of silverland, and although we do not claim to be a prophet . . . from what we have seen we are led to believe that this is no bubble, but founded on deposits of surpassing richness, and of an extent which long years of labor will not efface."

.

# 5

## Stampede to Meadow Lake 1866

In the spring the California legislature passed "An Act to Incorporate the Town of Meadow Lake," the law to become effective from and after June 13, 1866. A simplified measure jettisoned the excess baggage of the petitioners. Omitting mayor, aldermen, and so forth, the statute provided for a governing body of trustees, besides a marshal, treasurer, assessor, and poundmaster. These officers were to be elected on the second Wednesday in June, annually thereafter.

No sooner had the news reached town than a flock of would-be office-holders began tossing their hats into the ring. In a short time the list of candidates mounted up: 28 for marshal, 27 for treasurer, 19 for assessor, 11 for poundmaster. They became, one correspondent said, as " 'thick as autumn leaves in Vallombrosa.' . . . I counted one hundred and forty-nine aspirants for office. . . . within a fraction of one-half of the population." Candidacy was so popular, said another writer, that "The only ˉsensation I have witnessed since my stay here, was produced by . . . an eccentric individual who was announced as 'the man who didn't want office.' . . . Men, women, and even children . . . eagerly pressed forward . . . to catch a glimpse of this remarkable man." Homemade posters, declaring candidates' fitness for office, papered the town.

Incorporation and its trappings seemed important to the solid core of citizens who had stood by the town all winter, but these technicalities probably had little to do with the stampede to Meadow Lake. Beginning about the first of May, the rush was more explosive than that of the year before. Immigrants impatient to get in jammed every station in the vicinity. Saddle and pack trains, loaded with passengers and merchandise, plodded in hourly. Piles of provisions and furniture, awaiting transportation, were stacked up all along the way. The Central Pacific Railroad having been completed to Secret Canyon, travelers could ride to that point, then change to the Washoe stage or hoof it from the railhead. On stages from anywhere, seats had to be reserved days in advance. Over drifted trails from all directions trudged lines of gold-seekers, weird and faceless beings with their heads swathed in green veils to ward off snow blindness.

Old hands had recommended waiting until the weather moderated. The few partly dug-out roads were clogged again by heavy snowfall in late May, by another a week or so later, about six feet all told. Winter in this region did not give up easily. Not until the middle of June could stages get through from Nevada City; at that time town streets were clear, but then they were deep in mud. The lake was finally free of ice by the first week of July. "I would advise," said a man of experience, "all those who have plenty of money, and desire to learn the art of snow-shoe riding, to come out and stop awhile; but to those who are short of change, and can do anything where they are, they had better remain for the present. . . . there is no business of any kind going on, and there is no chance for a man to make a cent."

Sound advice like that had no effect. For two months adventurers poured in by the hundreds to swell the population to 4,000 or more. Many newcomers, disgusted with snow and cold, turned right around and went out again, but continual replacements caused no falling off of numbers. The town boiled. All hotels were packed, extra cots set up in halls and corners, every other sleeping place in town taken. Twenty or more men might be crowded into one room, appropriately called a corral. If a man who had a bed stayed out too late, he was likely to find his bunk preempted when he returned. Then he could walk the streets until dawn, curl up for chilly outdoor slumber on a bench or find shelter in a saloon—a face on the barroom floor.

Construction went on frantically, hampered, as it always had been, by shortage of lumber. Three sawmills, several miles away and isolated by snowbound roads, could not haul it in fast enough. Nevertheless within a month or two carpenters, in demand at $6 a day, ran up a good many buildings. The Andrews Hotel, Excelsior, and Lake House were enlarged; W. T. Warren was putting all the money he could scrape up into a two-story hotel. Messrs. Smith and Perkins planned to build a substantial stone structure, 30 feet by 80, at a cost of some $10,000. As for houses, a shell of thin boards, rustic outside, papered inside, and a ceiling of cotton domestic made a dwelling that could be knocked together in a hurry.

"It is almost impossible," said Orion Clemens, "to step off the street without climbing over a pile of lumber or running against a new house. . . . A man whom I have known a long time, and who, to my certain knowledge, can count a hundred, has counted sixty houses put up within the last two weeks . . . five new houses finished per day. At this rate, a man who desires to enjoy peace and quietness and rural walks, will have to leave the mountains."

Most of the inhabitants were not seeking peace and quiet. They delighted in the boom and hoped to take advantage of boom prices. Holders of desirable lots on B or C Street asked $1,500 to $3,000. The owner of choice corner property considered himself a wealthy man. Small business buildings rented for $200 to $300 a month. Borrowers who needed money could get it at an interest rate of 10% a month, provided they offered gilt-edged mining stocks as security. New arrivals had hardly brushed themselves off before they caught the fever of speculation, and began talking the language of lots, rents, and feet.

Feeding the hungry horde was a major problem. Freight wagons rolling in loaded with food managed to keep the supply adequate, but it lacked variety. No ham, fish, chickens, or cabbage, but enough potatoes, flour, bacon, molasses, and beef. Board at $12 a week was considered reasonable, though menus were hardly fancy enough to tempt a gourmet: breakfast, for example, price one dollar a la carte, was usually a biscuit, muddy coffee, and a steak as leathery as a miner's boot. One fellow said that a fire assay of Meadow Lake hash yielded these percentages: "Hair 7, Gum boots 3, Potatoes 60, Flies 2, Yellow jackets 1, Pork, very old 15, Beef 10, False teeth 2." The fare was ordinary, but old-timers thought that it was better than grub in the camps of '49.

The town revolved more dizzily than ever before: more and louder sawing and hammering, more miscellaneous uproar, more rushing around, more buzz. Men of long experience said that it reminded them of flush times during early stampedes on the Mother Lode. A correspondent observed: "Snow, 'feet,' candidates and nitroglycerine whisky constitute, at the present time, the prominent features of this place." Every bar was going full blast, every gambling place, all crowded every night and tumultuous with music, the jingle of gold and silver, faro, and bonhomie. At Jocelyn's Big Saloon, the Brilliant, cornetist Carl York and fellow musicians entertained throngs of convivial topers. The Gem Saloon, said a man of bohemian tastes, was "quite a gay little craft," where "the Ho Joe is warranted to inspire the immigrant's mind with energy enough to turn a boulder of granite into a beautiful quartz ledge." Asa Waugamann's bit-house, next door to the Excelsior Hotel, was another popular dispenser of the famous summit tipple.

The California Comedy Troupe, first professional company to visit the town, performed every night with mixed programs of plays—"Kiss in the Dark," "Christine"—music, and dancing.

Mrs. Mary Dramer, principal danseuse, was very popular. A spectator said that when she appeared in diaphanous drapery and "elevated her lower limb sufficiently high to form a parallel line with the floor, it elicited vociferous applause; but when her two limbs formed an obtuse angle, the delight of the audience knew no bounds." While a minister of the gospel was holding Sunday services in the improvised theater, an actor unaware of these proceedings strode on stage with a large poster advertising "Toodles and Love in Humble Life." The congregation was so well behaved that nobody laughed out loud, but there were muffled titters.

All of these occurrences were typical of a mining town on the make. It is worth remarking, however, that no correspondent mentioned any serious violence. Not a word about shootings or knifings or gouging barroom scuffles. That sort of thing had been so common in Virginia City that it shocked editors all over California, but it did not happen in Meadow Lake. The town might be a bedlam—mad, tipsy and reckless—but it was not bloodthirsty.

Elsewhere in the district, the upsurge made imaginative promoters project new towns. Ossaville was laid out on the trail to Polley's station two miles south of Meadow Lake, Enterprise City six miles away, Rocklin on Enterprise Hill, Carlisle and Paris near Old Man Mountain. There were rumors of others conceived but yet unborn. Whenever two or three cabins appeared in one place, that was a site for a town. Besides the emergent city of Meadow Lake itself, the region now had eight other would-be and hoped-for communities, all of which, one writer said, "bid fair to become lively business camps before the 'ides' of next November."

To keep pace with the rapid tempo and to live up to the prestige of Meadow Lake as a city-in-being, urban-minded citizens there organized the Excelsior Stock and Exchange Board. Alex Wightman, one of the instigators, became its President, George Vosburg its Secretary, William Perkins, Treasurer.

Among the thirty members were Whittemore, Friedman, J. K. Stuart, of the California Company, G. A. Brier, formerly of the Gold Hill *News,* and Orion Clemens.

Whittemore, the hotel man, immediately began to put up the Excelsior Building, corner of Second and O Streets, expressly as a headquarters for this body; the board room, in keeping with its importance, was to have a ceiling of planed lumber. Pending construction, the Board met elsewhere every day. A visitor who dropped in said that he was "forcibly reminded of the better days of Virginia. . . . the President . . . called the list of leading stocks with an emphasis which indicated the utmost confidence in their merit. . . . The list of mines . . . is now in the hands of the printer, and comprises two hundred and twenty-five claims."

The procedure looked like that of a big city Exchange, but there was something hollow about the performance, something like play-acting. The merits of the claims appeared to be in doubt. At least very little stock changed hands at the sessions and almost no money as the President read through the long list, from Antietam to Wisconsin. Low prices and few bids implied an attitude that was more like caution than utmost confidence: Calaveras, American Ledge, $11 asked, $2.50 bid; Gold Run, Phoenix Ledge, $18 asked, $5.37½ bid; Kentucky, Kentucky Ledge, $17 asked, $8 bid; and so on day after day, not more than half a dozen bids at each reading and only rarely a bid that met the asking price.

On most of those claims the only work done had been a little top scratching; not a single mine was a steady producer. All were unproved, merely names on elaborately printed certificates, handsome and impressive, but of uncertain value. The emptiness of the board room routine caused unfavorable newspaper comment and made the unregenerate snicker. Jokers hooted that the only stock this board dealt in was laughing-stock. Some critics said that since few Meadow Lake mines had been even partially developed, a Stock Board was premature. Others pointed out that it was likely to cause a mania of speculation and lead claim owners to believe that they could sell out without doing any work. Hence, people would conclude that the district was a calculated swindle.

One correspondent observed that the town had been "cursed with a mining stock board, composed of broken-down gamesters, whose efforts to force the market with wildcat have been signally abortive." Solemnly reading off names of mines that had hardly been opened did seem absurd make-believe, but it probably made Board members feel metropolitan. Perhaps it also lifted the spirits of other townsmen by confirming their belief that Meadow Lake was just as good as Virginia ever was —or San Francisco, for that matter.

Another boost to morale was the founding of a daily paper. The publishers, W. Lyon and E. B. Boust, had most of the press machinery brought in by mule train from Heaton's station. To transport a 500-pound casting of the Washington hand press, too heavy for any mule, they hired forty Chinese, who lugged it on long poles to a point somewhere near the town, then exhaustedly collapsed. Citizens were so eager to have a paper that they turned out in force to sledge in the big casting, spurring themselves on with a rousing chorus of "Marching Through Georgia."

Volume I, No. 1, of the Meadow Lake *Morning Sun* appeared on June 6, 1866. The editor was George W. Cassiday, late of the Dutch Flat *Enquirer*. "This morning," he said, "we launch our little bark upon the ocean of public opinion, hoping by upright and straight forward dealing to merit the approbation of those with whom we have to do." He also said that he intended to disseminate reliable mining information, expressed faith in "the superiority as well as the richness of our mines," and concluded with a promise of impartial treatment for everybody: "We are determined to make the SUN shed its genial rays upon all."

In the first number was a fine salutatory letter from a contributor named Joe Skinner. "This morning," he said, "a *new* SUN sheds its rays of light on us in our mountain home, among the snow-clad peaks of the Sierras, and may its glories never be dimmed by a cloud of adversity, but may it grow to be a SUN that shall send its rays of light to all parts of this great and glorious Republic, and may it also partake of the rich mineral wealth in which it is planted." The paper was off to a good start.

Columns of ads not only showed enthusiastic local support, but also gave an illuminating cross-sectional view of Meadow Lake business and professional affairs. Hotels bought space: Lake House, "Bed Rooms are Large, Airy and Comfortable"; Excelsior, "Comfort and Satisfaction"; St. Charles, Heatonville, Metropolitan, Monte Cristo, Continental, Andrews. Restaurants, too— "All the fat men, all the good natured men, and the best looking men in town board at the Capital Restaurant, C Street." Two physicians had cards in the paper, eight lawyers, four real estate and brokerage firms.

Grant's Passenger Service guaranteed "Safe and Trusty Animals for Ladies, and an accommodating Conductor sent with each train." Kilfoyl's Saddle and Express Train was on the job, J. McEldowney's Fast Freight Line, and Green and Company's Saddle Train, "Cheapest and Only Direct Route, Meadow Lake to Marysville." The Magnolia Billiard Saloon offered choice brandies and whiskies, and so did the Brilliant, Senate, Eureka, Gem, Nevada Exchange, Washington, Bank Exchange, Meadow Lake, Brokers' Exchange, and several other purveyors of nitroglycerine. Commission merchants were in business, three or four drygoods stores, house and sign painters, meat markets, notary publics, assayers, one jeweler and six breweries. If Meadow Lake was not yet a city, it had the accessories to become one.

The *Sun* rose just in time to report a quiet election of town officers, no rowdyism or ballot-box stuffing, 294 votes cast. New incumbents were: J. B. Jeffery, marshal; P. A. McCarty, assessor; R. Thompson, treasurer; and six trustees, Messrs. Starr, Rhue, Andrews, Kelsey, Vosburg and Jefferis. Nothing was said about a poundmaster. Perhaps that official was omitted as un-

## THE MORNING SUN,

Published every morning, (Sundays excepted.)

—BY—

**W. LYON & CO.**  w. LYON.

R. R. ROUTT.

OFFICE—On C street, Meadow Lake, Nevada
County, California.

SUBSCRIPTION:
Per Year, (by mail, or Express)..........$14 00
Six Months......................................8 00
Per Week, (Payable to the Carriers)......... .50

### PROFESSIONAL CARDS.

N. P. PATTERSON.    GEO. P. VOSBURG.

**PATTERSON & VOSBURG,**

STOCK BROKERS, REAL ESTATE AND
INSURANCE AGENTS.

Office—On B street, between 1st and 3d.

Conveyancing and Copying done with neatness
and dispatch.                                    1-tf

**W. BERGMANN, M. D.,**

PHYSICIAN AND SURGEON,

(Formerly of Carson, Nevada)

Particular attention paid to Operative Surgery
and Venereal Disease.

Can be found for the present at H. Ruhe's on
A street, or at the Lake House.                  1-tf

**DR. ALFRED WEHLER,**

SURGEON AND PHYSICIAN.

OFFICE—On B street, opposite the Excelsior
Brewery.                                         1-tf

Keeps constantly on hand and for sale every
variety of Drugs and Medicines.                  1-tf

**GALLOWAY & COWDEN,**

ATTORNEYS AT LAW,

Office—Next door north of the Lake House.  1tf
FRANK TILFORD..................J. C. FOSTER.

**TILFORD & FOSTER,**

ATTORNEYS AT LAW,

## STOCK BROKERS AND MINING AGENTS.

**BILLET & BRIER,**

....AND....

General Agents.

REAL ESTATE AND STOCK BROKERS

MEMBERS OF THE EXCELSIOR STOCK
AND EXCHANGE BOARD.

Office—on C street, between Second and Third.

For Sale or Lease!

HOUSES AND LOTS IN ALL PARTS OF
THE CITY.

Mining Stocks Bought and Sold.

MINING COMPANIES INCORPORATED

....AND....

Stock Books Furnished.

REAL ESTATE AND MINING DEEDS,

Affidavits,    Contracts,    Leases,

And all Legal Papers,

DRAWN WITH NEATNESS AND DESPATCH

## FREIGHT AND PASSENGER TRAINS.

STAGE AND SADDLE TRAIN,

From

*MEADOW LAKE TO MARYSVILLE,*

Via *JACKSON'S RANCH, CAMPTONVILLE,
AND BROWN'S VALLEY.*

CHEAPEST AND ONLY DIRECT ROUTE!

Through Tickets.................$16

Passengers taken by this saddle train to Jackson's Ranch, thence, by stage, to Marysville and
all intermediate points.

For tickets, &c., apply at Andrews' Hotel, corner of A and second streets.

GREEN & CO., Proprietors.
1tf    J. C. BERWICK, Agent.

**GRANT'S PASSENGER TRAIN,**

OFFICE AT THE EXCELSIOR HOTEL.

From Polley's to Meadow Lake.

**Through in the Quickest Time.**

Leave Polley's Station on the arrival of the
Pioneer Company's stage the Excelsior Hotel in time
to connect with the stages from Sacramento.

Returning leave the Excelsior Hotel in time
to connect with the stages from Sacramento.

SAFE and TRUSTY ANIMALS for LADIES
And an accommodating Conductor sent with
each train.

All orders left with B. F. Whittemore, of the
Excelsior Hotel will be promptly attended to.
1-tf    A. GRANT, Proprietor.

**KILFOYL'S**

SADDLE AND EXPRESS TRAIN!

....FROM....

Meadow Lake to Bear Valley,

*ONLY DIRECT ROUTE* TO *NEVADA CITY,
GRASS VALLEY AND MARYSVILLE.*

THE Undersigned would respect-
fully announce that he has established and
is now running a tri-weekly Saddle and Express
Train from Meadow Lake, via Baltimore and
Old Man Mountain, to Bear Valley connecting
with the Pioneer Stage Company, reaching
Nevada City, Grass Valley, Marysville, and all
intermediate points.

Passengers by this route, to or from Nevada
City, can rely on being taken through in one
day.

## HOTELS, RESTAURANTS, SALOONS.

, LAKE HOUSE RESTAURANT.

HAVING Leased and Refitted the
LAKE HOUSE DINING ROOM,
I design keeping a

First Class Restaurant,

And I feel confident of being able to please all
who may favor me with a call.

CHAS. H. COBB,
1 tf    Proprietor.

**EXCELSIOR HOTEL**

B. F. WHITTEMORE.    F. P. MEDICAN.

....AND....

GENERAL STAGE HOUSE,

Corner of C and Second streets, Meadow Lake.

WILL be conducted as a First Class
House. Close and strict attention on the
part of the Proprietors, to their business, will
insure to their guests

Comfort and Satisfaction.

MEALS PREPARED AT ALL HOURS.

Stage and Passenger Trains arrive and depart
from the house daily.

Passengers booked to any part of this State or
Nevada.

## EXCELSIOR.

[WRITTEN FOR THE MEADOW LAKE MORNING SUN.]

Up where Sierra's lofty summits rise,    [skies—
Whose glittering domes magnetic touch the
Where nature in her wildest robe is drest,
Wearing in summer, still her fleecy vest;
For winter holds full long her rigid sway,
And emerald spring was never known to stay,
And but reluctant Flora deigns, with grim,
Softening the aspect of so wild a scene—
Excelsior stands—and no vain boast the name,
For soon these snow cased huts shall rise to fame;
Here every rugged hill its treasure shows,
And only walls the hardy miners' blows.
For here we see, in mountain's granite side,
For here the source—yes, here the vast supply
Of Yuba's wealth, the truth is now so plain
No lingering doubt can ever more remain.
A golden circle here we well may claim,
For each wild hill doth boundless wealth contain,
And mines of opals, diamonds each and rare,
Before unknown, these granite walls all bear.
Yes, here dame nature's store house we've found,
Though guarded well with walls of snow around,
But nature's guards and shields of snow are vain
Each barrier down, and scattered by his hands.
With patience for his aid, he conquering stands,
But one short year since first these mines were
Behold, like magic, lo! a town is shown; [known,
Through the long storms of cruel, spotless snow,
A thousand hands have daily fought the foe,
The bold Sierran Mountain's beard, they've torn
away—

His heart they'll pearce and drag it to the day;
From his old veins a golden stream shall flow,
And Meadow Lake a mighty city grow.    WALP.

Meadow Lake City, June 7, 1866.

## REMINISCENCE OF EARLY TIMES IN CALIFORNIA.

Most forty-niners remember old Green-
wood, the mountaineer. He had been a
hunter and trapper from boyhood—one of
those men who always kept to the westward
of civilization, and, very unwilling on
their part, prepare the wilderness, in some
degree, for its coming. He had hunted
across the continent in days when from the
Missouri river to the Bay of San Francisco
was *terra incognito*, and in his old age found
himself, with his Indian wife and troop of

necessary, nothing much to impound here but deer and woodchucks. On the day after the election the winning candidates
got out the band, rounded up the losers and paraded through
town carrying banners made of campaign posters, "after which,"
said the *Sun,* "the would-be officials were escorted to the lake
and shipped to the head-waters of Salt River in a flat-boat. The
best of feeling prevailed."

The trustees promptly formulated a number of ordinances
about duties of officers, licensing of restaurants, lodging houses
and saloons, road and poll taxes, penalties for offenses like
drunkenness, resisting arrest, shooting, racing in the streets.
They allowed the marshal $150 a month, the assessor $8 a day,
engaged a clerk for themselves at $75 a month, created the
office of town surveyor, and engaged a small police force. When
they proposed a forty-man fire company, to be called Excelsior
Company No. 1, townsmen contributed $744 to buy a fire engine.

The assessor got busy assessing. Marshal Jeffery soon made
his first arrest, moving in on a street fight and collaring two men
to the cheers of an admiring crowd. Thus the machinery of an
incorporated town began to move with dispatch, but the cost
of keeping it going looked as if it might be hard on taxpayers.
The trustees found that out; before long they began to negotiate
for loans to meet the payroll.

Yet they regarded borrowing as only a temporary expedient
to tide them over until the time when ample funds would be
pouring in. The gold rush, continuing with unabated velocity,
seemed to assure general well-being. The *Sun* estimated an influx of five to ten thousand by the first of July. "Arrivals from
all parts of California and Nevada," said a correspondent in mid-
June, "are daily increasing, and averaged last week some fifty
per day." They were a variegated lot. One observer divided
them into three categories: "Distinguished arrivals—editors,
doctors, theologians and speculators not a few; notorious arrivals—chaingang graduates, bummers, vagrants and idlers in
countless numbers; ordinary arrivals—miners, mechanics and
laborers generally."

In about two weeks the industrious ones staked off over 500 claims, the alluring prospects producing the usual quota of imaginary millionaires. Hardly anybody was too modest to consider his holdings worth less than a hundred thousand or so. The *Sun's* news heads were in the proper vein of booming confidence: "Rich Rock," "Buildings Going Up," "Richer Than Ever," "Struck It," "New Discovery." Orion Clemens, under the pseudonym of Noiro, discussed the potential prosperity of the region in eleven long articles he wrote for the paper on "Our Ledges."

Yet mining news, spotty and not very brilliant, made suspicious editors wonder whether mine superintendents were suppressing information on cleanups that were disappointing. Concern over the difficulties of separating gold from other metals was more in evidence than heretofore. A few knowledgeable experts were beginning to suspect that they did not get the gold because it was not there to get, that Meadow Lake ledges were of low value, that veins rich on the surface pinched out somewhere below. These shocking surmises were not broadcast at the time.

Of three completed quartz mills, the Enterprise had been written off as a failure, and the Winton was not doing much. The California mill crushed four tons of rocks that yielded $159.91. Not spectacular. But the California people apparently believed that they were doing well enough, for they entertained at an open house. The editor of the *Sun,* who attended, said that he followed a devious route through the ore room to the amalgamating room, where he found "all kinds of refreshments, among which were various kinds of cakes and a bounteous supply of lager, whisky (not Ho Joe), and cigars." The early flowering of the corporation cocktail party, no cheap drinks either, evidently meant that the California outfit thought it was on the way to getting out of the red.

The Excelsior Company began to build a 20-stamp mill, which would be equipped with the most up-to-date pans, agitators and concentrators, all the newest devices for treating stubborn ores, the works to be ready by August at a cost of about $100,000. Some $20,000 of that price had to be applied only to transportation, the high figure showing the expense of any operation in this mountainous country.

About 300 men were reported to be employed in the mines; forecasters predicted that by early autumn the number would be at least 2,000. As usual, the crying need was money for opening claims and for more mills. Roads were needed, too. The district was still hard to get into, still hard to get around in. Extensive dead-work of the previous year was yet unfinished. Said the *Sun*: "We might walk over ledges more valuable than Peru or Potosi ever boasted, and not be a dollar richer for the wealth beneath our feet, unless capital should come to our aid. . . . Individual efforts may *prospect,* but companies, regularly organized, must *develop* mines." At various times capitalists from San Francisco and elsewhere were reported to be snooping around and making encouraging noises, but seeming to be in no hurry to loosen purse strings. A good deal of capital had already been poured into the place, yet either it was not enough or, considering meager returns, it had not been wisely spent. Practical men were saying that it was foolish to build a town and quartz mills before having worked the mines.

The district, said a Washoe editor, "is a very poor place for a poor man to go at present, for there are hundreds of men who cannot get employment." Many men had no money to work claims, and others, of the bummer fraternity, did not want to work at anything. Not a few had been led on by the delusion, common to every gold rush, that a fortune could be gathered in without much effort. By the end of June the flow of newcomers had slowed down to about thirty a day. Probably the total number of arrivals was close to the *Sun's* predicted ten thousand, but most of them did not stay long.

In July correspondents, who had an eye for such statistics, figured that more people were leaving than were coming in. Papers in valley towns made sarcastic remarks about "an ephemeral city," "that summer retreat for white bears," "snow-burg." One editor observed: "We know of several good fellows who have struck 'good things' in that vicinity, none of whom have made any better strikes than such as *struck out* for other parts." Travelers returning from the summit reported that the town was too far ahead of the mines, and that all kinds of business there, except mining, was overdone.

Yet departures appeared to cause little letup in congestion and commotion at Meadow Lake. The town was still crowded, though people were somewhat at loose ends. "The majority of the population," said a letter-writer, "seem to have no other occupation but sitting around hotels and saloons in chairs, when they are lucky enough to find seats." The whole situation was like that of the year before: nearly everybody took for granted the great wealth of the ledges, but nobody was getting enough out of them to keep up with board and bar bills.

In the early summer of 1866 the town hesitated between advance toward higher tide and the ebb of recession. The pause was momentary, for a gold town did not stand still: it moved ahead or fell back. Between the forward and the retrograde was an instant in time, the dividing line sharp as a knife edge. Reaction set in imperceptibly almost before anybody knew that the thrust of momentum had spent itself. So it was at Meadow Lake. Flush times there were brief and misleading, in that they were not kept going by the stimulus of gold production. The illusion of prosperity flourished on the money immigrants brought in with them. When funds were exhausted, and credit too, the flush subsided.

Yet the old familiar optimism was strong. The *Sun* proudly reported progress: "One year ago . . . . there was not a house to be seen, and not more than two hundred persons. . . . To-day we have near six hundred buildings, and a population of between two and three thousand. . . . three quartz mills completed, and several others under construction," a new toll road that "will place us within two hours ride of the cars as soon as completed, and this will be within fifty days." Another undaunted fellow foresaw a glorious future. Reflecting upon the hitherto untrodden wilderness of the Sierras, he said that "Before another year shall have rolled around, their solitudes shall echo the mingled clang of ponderous machinery, the shrill whistle of steam engines, and the shriek and roar of the flying Iron Horse."

As always, nothing blighted the high spirits of the 500 or so people who looked upon themselves as permanent residents. They manifested their enthusiasm and their faith in homespun poems that found a haven in the *Sun.* One versifier wrote: "Near a calm Lake, all margined round with green,/Softening the aspect of so wild a scene—/Excelsior stands—and no vain boast the name,/For soon these snow cased huts shall rise to fame." Another exclaimed: "Excelsior! Excelsior! thy wide spreading fame,/A wild charm has wrought 'round thy magical name,/Like a halo of glory encircling the head/Of a queen in her beauty, just blushingly wed." These poets were not ready to give up their town as a lost cause.

Townspeople enjoyed all kinds of entertainment, homemade and professional. Wormer's magic-lantern show made a hit, billed as "New Exhibition of the Great Stereoscopticon!!! and California and Nevada Scenery! Produced by the wonderful and Celebrated Magnetian Lights." When Major General William S. Rosecrans paid a visit in late June, citizens turned out to welcome the Civil War veteran. Trustees tendered him the freedom of the city, escorted him over several ledges and, although the record fails to mention it, no doubt halted somewhere to refresh the old soldier with restoratives.

Dancers kept on dancing. The Masonic Ball on June 25 outshone all previous social events. The ballroom, in the new addition of the Andrews Hotel, was festooned with evergreen boughs, bouquets, and Masonic regalia. Music, by a new string ensemble of six pieces, was "under the able leadership of George Edmonds," said the *Sun,* "and certainly the most fastidious could not have wished for better.... at least one hundred persons shared in the amusement—about forty of whom belonged to the gentler sex." At midnight they took time out for the customary supper. Then the music struck up again, and the dancers, with renewed energy, swirled around until daylight.

The men, women and children—some ninety-five youngsters under the age of fifteen—who thought of Meadow Lake as their home were not muscle-bound, physically or temperamentally. If they were avid for gold, that urge seemed less important than an infectious joie de vivre. They were not afflicted with emotional hardening of the arteries, they were not downhearted, and they savored life.

# 6

XXXXXXXXXXXXX

# Sierra Summer 1866

MIDSUMMER in the high Sierras was benevolent, a gracious recompense for long months of snow and ice. It was like early spring in lower country, exhilarating with the beauty of perennial rebirth. Under a kindly sun, warm but not oppressive, summit meadows deep in grass, new and bright green, blossomed with a great variety of fragrant wildflowers. They colored glens and slopes and braved the higher reaches of the mountains. Dark hues of fir and cedar looked lighter, moss-covered granite less grim. The editor of the *Sun* became rhapsodic. "All the hillsides and little valleys in the vicinity of our town," he said, "are now as blooming as the rose or a toper's nose. . . . All our little valleys are at this season fresh and Spring-like. In many of the most elevated, the grass is just starting and the little Alpine flowers just peeping out."

In this vernal time the band resumed its nightly concerts from out on the lake off the Plaza, delighting picnickers with songs and serenades. Another kind of evening concert was the croaking of a myriad of frogs in the many ponds all around. People who developed a taste for frog legs went on spearing expeditions with table forks tied to the ends of long poles. Some fellows, flat broke, found this food a life-saver.

The nautically-minded cruised up and down Meadow Lake

in a fleet of sailboats. Two hundred and fifty spectators gathered to watch *Blue Bird* win from *Eclipse* in a spirited race for a purse of $20. One tragedy marred the sailing. When a skipper trying to come about near the Yuba dam capsized his boat, a woman and her four-year-old daughter were drowned. Theirs were the first deaths to be reported from Meadow Lake.

Dan De Quille came back to town, not as a reporter this time but only as a sociable being returning to one of his favorite spots to enjoy reunion with old Washoe friends. The visit was such an agreeable round of treating and being treated that a story in the Virginia *Union*, probably written by Alf Doten, said that "Dan is now engaged with Brier and Parker who have organized a club for the destruction of all 'Ho Joe.' At last accounts they were all very busy, and from appearances, have been at work quite diligently."

Pleasurable doings, combining the amenities of country club and marina, belied the recession that had subdued the district. The town was dull, correspondents said, people still leaving, business desultory, outlook dim, the mines gone up. Once-filled hotels had plenty of empty rooms now, restaurants no crowds elbowing in for hash, merchants no press of customers, streets no clutter of pedestrians and swearing mule drivers impatient to get somewhere. Unnatural calm descended as the pace became slower and more listless, the erstwhile music and hilarity of the town's night spots muted and forlorn. Men with long faces gloomily wondered what to do next.

By early August a thousand or more had pulled out. The numerous floaters among them were no loss, for their departure reduced the number of loafers hanging around. "Everybody that can get away from here is doing so," said a letter-writer, "and if your correspondent had enough coin to purchase a 'square meal,' he would 'get up and git' also." They seemed to be as frenzied about getting out as they had been to get in. Mining shares went down until they were practically worthless. Carpenters and wood sawyers lost their jobs when the scramble to put up hotels and stores slacked off, although Smith and Perkins were going ahead with their splendid stone building. Rentals declined sharply, and high prices of lots plummeted to $400 or less, building and lot together for the cost of materials and labor, but no buyers stepped forward. Those who had put all their ready cash into real estate and houses faced ruinous losses.

Disgusted men drifting down from the mountains spread unflattering opinions. At Grass Valley, center of one of the richest gold sections in California, the editor of the *Union* said that every day "we see men returning from this new gold field pronouncing it a humbug—the same men who . . . were ready to stake all they possessed that Meadow Lake during the present season would be a larger town than Grass Valley or Nevada, and that inside of two years the Excelsior District would be turning out more gold than Grass Valley Township." Other disgruntled returnees called Meadow Lake "the biggest bilk in the world. . . . No money, no mining sales, and no work in progress." One disillusioned adventurer, who had been in the forefront of fortune-hunters up there, vehemently expressed himself in verse: "At Huffaker's he last was seen/Imbibing nitroglycerine, /And as he quaffed each fiery dram/In accents wild he cried, 'God damn/Excelsior!' "

City fathers and paid police became luxuries Meadow Lake townsmen could not afford. Having second thoughts about the wisdom of incorporation, they called a meeting and voted 250 to 93 in favor of dispensing with officials and their salaries. They also voted 173 to 36 against levying a school tax. The trustees announced that when they had discharged a municipal debt of about $1,000, they would repeal ordinances concerning collection of revenue, and suspend formal government. Thus, within two months of its establishment, incorporation was on the way out, its going recommended by the same people who had urged it in the first place. Yet it did not cease at once. Perhaps the trustees had trouble liquidating the debt, for they were still formulating ordinances a year later, and town officers were still on duty. Adopting immediate economy measures, they cut the marshal's salary to $50 a month and abolished the pay of the town clerk.

In keeping with a general tightening of the belt, the *Sun* reduced publication to semi-weekly, then to weekly, and the Excelsior Stock and Exchange Board quietly disbanded without having become acclimated to the impressive board room, 40 feet by 72, readied by Whittemore. Elsewhere in the district most of the towns, founded with high hopes but hardly well started, went to pieces at once. A sardonic letter-writer who jogged over to the few houses and whiskey shops called Paris remarked that "The *bourse* was flat at the time of our visit; *rentes* not over $10 a month. We rode along the *boulevards,* stopped at the *Hotel des Invalides,* inquired of several of our American friends how long they had been on the continent, galloped through the *Bois Bolognes,* visited the *Champs Elysees,* (Warfield's Ranch vulgarly called) and made our grand exit without dispatching a hasty plate of soup with the Parisiens."

Within a week or two of the high point of the stampede, boom degenerated to a state of affairs that looked like bust. Yet Meadow Lake, if down, was not defunct. The town was not dead, only half-dead, groggy and dazed but still breathing. One sign of life was a company authorized to install a water system of reservoirs a hundred feet higher than the town, pipes laid in streets, hydrants at intervals for fire protection. The trustees had matter-of-factly enacted Ordinance No. 15 granting this company the right to proceed. Plans were being formulated as if the place were humming with business, as if good times coming meant thousands of residents calling for water.

Another flicker of animation was the opening of Snyder's New Music Hall in mid-August. The management announced that every Tuesday evening "will be set apart for an exclusive Dramatic Entertainment for the accommodation of ladies and families, when the popular artists, Mrs. Lavinia H. Beatty and Mr. L. F. Beatty, will appear in a sterling play," supported by

Mrs. Mary Dramer, George Edmonds, Charles Lovell and other talented performers. Mrs. Beatty, called "Excelsior's favorite," starred as Pauline in *The Lady of Lyons;* Mr. Beatty, "one of California's most gifted actors," as Claude Melnotte.

If some towns in the district had disintegrated, others were about to spring up, at least according to a correspondent of the Virginia *Union.* He said that prospectors who had discovered coal oil six miles away were laying off a town called Petroliaville. In another spot a man named Jones was said to have planned a community to be known as Kerosene City. These things were possible, even credible, yet the tale sounds as if that correspondent were giving free play to his imagination. At any rate, no such places ever got on the map.

Then, early in August while the district was staggering in the doldrums of letdown, astonishing news burst upon Meadow Lake. The free gold in 29 tons of ore from the Mohawk and Montreal mine produced a bar of 52 ounces worth over $800. This chunk of bullion, yellow and lovely, was on display at Collins' hat store on Second Street, where it could be seen and touched and marveled over—the first tangible result of much horrendous labor. Everybody dropped in for a good long look at this fascinating object.

The effect was as exhilarating as the first swallow of Ho Joe. "We cannot but notice," said the *Sun,* "the change in the countenances and feelings of our citizens . . . . Men who for days past had given way to despair, and lost all confidence in our mines, seem to awaken from their lethargy . . . . we overheard a crowd of these despairing individuals exulting over their good fortune in having at last found the right country." Perhaps this district might turn out to be the big thing, after all.

The *Sun* also said that at least two hundred claims showed an abundance of free gold, and that if each of them got out fifty tons of ore, conservatively valued at $30 a ton, the yield should be $300,000, "more actual money than has ever been in the district from its birth." Although that cash was not forthcoming, the gold brick appeared to settle the vexing question of whether or not stubborn Meadow Lake ores could be profitably worked. "Now," said the *Sun*, "it is proven beyond a doubt that our mines will pay, we shall look for our miners to go to work as though they wished to assist in the development of the district." Proof was not beyond doubt because of refractory sulphurets. Always present in the rock from any mine, they would not give in to the usual milling processes of crushing and amalgamating. How to get the gold out of them was a problem yet unsolved.

Nevertheless, as if to confirm the assertion of proof, a second gold bar appeared at the Wells Fargo office, this one a bit small, valued at only $384, but undeniably gold. That was followed by others, a dozen being shipped out during August. The *Sun* for the first time published figures on bullion for the month: from the Mohawk and Montreal, Mountaineer, U. S. Grant and others, a total of $5,015.37. Compared with weekly bullion shipments from Virginia of about $150,000, the Meadow Lake output was meager, but it was a start and as a morale-builder superb. "Let those who are interested in Meadow Lake take heart," said a California editor. "The era of 'show and blow' has passed away, and given place to energetic labor."

A show of genuine gold made the boys spunky. They clashed in a number of spirited fist fights that were encouraging signs of an improved frame of mind—not vindictive encounters apparently, but merely sparring matches to release energy. The *Sun* gave the results of one bout at the Brilliant saloon: "Pealed noses, 1; mashed hand, 1; mashed stove pipe joints, 2; broken stove legs, 4."

Even while some disillusioned critics were muttering about general slowdown, mining affairs took a sudden upturn. Idlers and speculators having left town, the workers got down to business. They prospected energetically and all day long shattered silence with thunderous blasts, making holes like rifle pits in ledges every few feet. An onlooker said that he could not raise the color in most of these dents, but that drawback did not halt furious assaults on the hard granite. The shaft at the Enterprise ledge was down fifty feet.

Seven quartz mills were now completed or going up. The Excelsior mill, that was supposed to have been ready by the first of August, finally began running on the 29th of September. A correspondent of the Virginia *Union* lyrically reported the event: "After the lacing up of belts, tightening up of nuts, putting in screens, etc., the steam was turned on, the great flywheel commenced to turn, and the whole mill in a moment appeared a thing of life, and the noise incident to the commotion of the machinery was like unto sweet music to the ear of the toiling miner, the melodious strains of which are so agreeable to those who delve for the rich minerals that lie in their midst, that they are content to still labor on, being assured that their reward is within their grasp." After a sendoff like that, the Excelsior would not dare to fail; at once the mill began crushing forty tons of rock a day.

A man named Deetken experimented with a chlorination process to extract gold from sulphurets, and a man named Riggs tried a desulphurizing process. In the air was talk of building a number of reduction plants that were designed to break down refractory ores. Data on rock-crushing and assays came out in a profusion reminiscent of the previous year: fifty tons of Enterprise ore yielded $1,210; forty-eight tons of Mohawk and Montreal, $2,233.02; an assay of Enterprise sulphurets showed $1,231 to the ton; a U. S. Grant cleanup returned $2,718 in free gold; Shooting Star rock assayed $624.24 in gold per ton; nineteen pack mules, loaded with ore from the Aurora claim, passed through Nevada City; and so on and so on. The *Sun* reported bullion shipments for September as $4,121.32; for October, $6,674.78.

The flurry of action improved the general attitude toward the district. "In every fever," said a correspondent, "there is a crisis, upon which hangs the death or convalescence of the patient. Meadow Lake has just passed that critical stage. . . ."

The editor of the *Sun* had no doubts about restoration of health. "We have built up a substantial and handsome town," he said, "and paid for it. We have opened three excellent roads . . . we have constructed six good mills." (The seventh mill, the Enterprise, had been remodeled, but it was not a good mill.)

In terms of material achievement, he had reason for pride. By autumn of 1866 the town had over 600 houses and other buildings, the district four sawmills and close to one hundred miles of stage roads, rough but navigable, with stations and stables along the way. All these things, together with quartz mills, had come into being in about fifteen months at a cost of probably well beyond $2,000,000. The speed was astounding, the staggering expense evidence of tremendous faith, also of the long distance mining returns had yet to go before they matched that outlay.

Summer, beautiful but brief, continued to be temperate and refreshing, but it was moving on toward a more uncertain season. One of the disadvantages of high Sierras country was the short time favorable to mining work or any other kind of outdoor labor—about three to four months between the melting snow of one winter and the new snow of the next one. A number of merchants, forestalling the approach of bad weather, packed up their stocks of goods and set out for lower and milder levels. Store buildings that had commanded high rents were offered free to tenants who would take care of the property. The departure created an unusual stir that was lively but saddening, too. Other citizens who were also taking off for warmer climes reduced the Meadow Lake population to a remnant that remained to battle winter storms at the summit. Among the stayers, a smaller number than that of the year before, were such steadfast adherents as Brumsey, Friedman, Whittemore and, assuredly, Henry Hartley.

If only a corporal's guard, the group was compact and, as usual, eager, interested in whatever was going on. One event was the arrival of Miss Eliza A. Pittsinger, who came to town in October. Hailed as "the talented poetess of the Pacific coast" and "a poetess of great genius," she appeared at the Metropolitan Hotel in programs of recitations described as "chaste drawing room readings." One querulous fellow complained that her voice was monotonous and thin, pronunciation faulty and articulation indistinct, but he was probably a curmudgeon. The *Sun* praised without reserve. The entertainment, said the paper, "excelled, by far, anything of the kind we have been permitted to hear in the mountains. . . . Miss Pittsinger has but few, if any, superiors in the art of elocution. Her readings of the comic poems, the Yankee ballad, Napoleon's visit to Moscow, was such as to make the audience roar with laughter. Her delivery of Poe's master piece, the Raven, was with the greatest taste."

Especially admired were her original poems inspired by the Civil War and published as *Bugle Peals*. One of these that she read at the Metropolitan was "The Eagle": "Oh, thou child in shadows roaming, I will give you now an omen—/I will give you here a lesson that you ne'er have heard before;/See these STARS in glory blending—to a radiant center tending—/See their azure brightness lending to your country's future store" and so forth. That poem, said an enthusiastic critic, "has gained for the author an extended reputation," for it "breathes a pure patriotism."

Miss Pittsinger was so delighted with Sierra country that she later celebrated its beauty in fervent prose. "Enchanting region!" she exclaimed; "thine Autumnal robes were decked with grace and loveliness, reflecting from their golden textures hues as soft as were thy skies, gorgeous as the beams of thy noon-day sun, and grand as the majestic reign of thy midnight moon—and yet 'tis said thy Summer robes were far more beautiful than these; 'tis said thy sloping hills were bedecked with flowers of most surpassing loveliness—that thy placid Lake arose to a grander level, and thy thoroughfares were filled with much of the Grace, Beauty, and Wealth of the Land." If the final remark was a slight overstatement, the tribute was nevertheless a splendid one, and well deserved it was.

A less complimentary visitor who dropped in for an overnight stay in late October was Mark Twain. He came in, he said, "over a villainous road, which usually led through beautiful and picturesque mountain scenery, variegated with taverns, where they charge reasonable rates for dinners and get them up satisfactorily." Headed for Virginia, he was on his first speaking tour, but he did not stay in Meadow Lake long enough to deliver his lecture on the Sandwich Islands.

Yet he looked around, amazed at what he saw. Like others, he was impressed by the grandeur of the region, but the town, he remarked, was "the wildest exemplar of speculation I have ever stumbled upon. Here you find Washoe recklessness and improvidence repeated." Relying on substantial returns from ledges promising but unopened, "they have built a handsome town and painted it neatly and planned long wide streets, and got ready for a rush of business, and then—jumped aboard the stage coaches and deserted it! . . . Here is a really handsome town, built of two-story frame houses—a town capable of housing 3,000 persons with ease, and how many has it got? A hundred! You can have a house all to yourself merely by promising to take care of it. . . . A bright, new, pretty town all melancholy and deserted, and yet showing not one sign of decay or dilapidation. I never saw the like before!"

If Meadow Lake was not quite deserted, it was almost so, the population much too sparse to fill the place, no traffic on the streets, a hush hanging over the whole town. The silence and the emptiness were eerie. Hotels were closing, the ownership of some of them changing hands. The noise of blasting was seldom heard, and the sale of many claims gave notice that the sellers were quitting the district.

The outlook seemed anything but bright, yet champions were not wanting. One correspondent, admitting that Meadow Lake was hardly an up-and-coming spot at the moment, said: "I verily believe that another Spring will witness unwonted activity in the mines hereabouts, and that within a few months from the beginning of fair weather in 1867, this mining campaign will . . . eclipse any on the Pacific coast. I do most positively assure you that rich ledges are here, and they require a reasonably large expenditure of capital . . . to bring forth mighty dividends from 'Excelsior.' " Even Mark Twain, listening to the opinions of mining men, modified his views somewhat. "It is expected," he said, "that the camp will be as lively and populous as ever in the Spring."

# 7

## Uncertain Year 1866–67

THE MOST DRAMATIC EVENT of late autumn, 1866, was a mining fracas, the first of its kind in this district. When the Golden Eagle Company struck a good ledge, the Excelsior Company maintained that it had prior right to the ground, but the Golden Eagle, ignoring that claim, began to put up a quartz mill at the mine. Whereupon Excelsior stalwarts, in a raid by night, tore down the framework, burned lumber and destroyed miscellaneous property lying around. When workmen arrived in the morning, they were confronted by the Excelsior president, secretary, superintendent and two other men standing guard with drawn pistols. Bad trouble seemed imminent, but no fight occurred and no shooting, workers retreating in good order. The upshot was a warrant for the arrest of the vandals, who were promptly apprehended by a constable.

After a two-day trial, attended by a crowded roomful of spectators, the jury brought in a verdict against the Excelsior Company. The judge fined each officer $100, the first assistant $50 and the fifth man $25. Unable to pay their fines or to furnish bail, the culprits were consigned to an improvised lockup. The episode demonstrated that, though incorporation might now be unpopular, some sort of constabulary and a J. P. were needed to keep the peace and to settle disputes.

Townsmen were so well pleased with the verdict that they celebrated by making a night of it on copious drafts of lager and Ho Joe. The next day, in an admirable display of the co-operative spirit notwithstanding morning-after blues, they sent out two six-horse wagons loaded with lumber and about fifteen carpenters who had volunteered their services gratis to rebuild the Golden Eagle mill.

Not long afterward a more disastrous occurrence was the worst fire so far, when the Excelsior bakery and Zerger's store, together with its entire stock of goods, burned to the ground. That 40-man fire company that had been proposed had apparently died a-borning, for it was not mentioned in dispatches, nor was the fire engine for which citizens had contributed $744. Those water hydrants were not in place either. Volunteers being ineffectual, the fire blazed away unchecked, as it was likely to do through the whole town some day.

Winter weather held off for awhile, then in late November struck hard with an eleven-day storm that piled up ten feet of snow on the Plaza. December produced eight days of rain, twenty days of snow, blizzards one after another until the additional fall became inconsequential to beleaguered inhabitants. The town disappeared under drifts of twenty to thirty feet or more. A traveler who snowshoed in from Cisco arrived at the place where he thought Meadow Lake should be, but all he could see was a waste of polar white. Then he was startled when a man suddenly popped up out of the snow. "Where is Meadow Lake?" asked the visitor. "Why," said the man, "you are right on the Plaza."

Travel, except by snowshoe, was too difficult to attempt without urgent reason. A horseback rider could get through to Pierce's station, 16 miles away, in eight hours, or to Cisco in less time, but there were no stages, sledges, or pack trains. Fairly regular mail service kept news of the town in the papers of other places, though Zack's Snowshoe Express was not on duty this time.

Residents did not seem to mind being cut off. Not lonely or more than momentarily oppressed by isolation, they adapted themselves with astonishing ease to the chill half-light of a strange subterranean life. They crawled in and out of their homes by second-story windows or skylights, and through the deep snow that packed the streets dug tunnels from house to house. The elaborate surface entrance to the store of Adams and Johnson was a round hole that had a frozen spiral stairway winding around it. One man put up over his property a notice reading "This House and Lot for Sale," and added, "Inquire down the chimney."

People sat out storms within doors. They kept fires roaring, wrote letters, visited each other, ducking through crystal caverns that flashed brilliantly in the light of lanterns, and got up impromptu dancing parties. Like miners in the camps of '49, they read whatever they could lay their hands on, passing around well-thumbed books, journals old and new, perusing the weekly *Sun* several times over, even the long-standing ads.

On clear days everybody, young and old, surfaced for their favorite sport of snowshoeing. Neophytes sprawled and experts sped down right over the top of the Andrews Hotel of two and a half stories. The ladies, as usual, took the masculine eye. "Nothing on a bright sunshiny morning," said one bedazzled gentleman, "can be more graceful or beautiful than a fair young lassie gliding with Sylph like motions over hills and plains upon her Norwegian shoes." Another entranced observer remarked: "Talk about a divine creature on Plimpton's roller skates—that is nothing compared to the sylph-like form of an angel as she gracefully swoops down from her aerie on Norwegian snowshoes." Those sylph-like girls must have been good.

Racing became a daily program, Judge Tilford acting as umpire, who was accused of always favoring the sylphs in a mixed contest. Fourteen men competed in a race of 500 yards from the summit of a steep hill. The winner was S. Chambers, time 23 seconds. Winner of the ladies' event was Miss Clara

Head, whom an enraptured spectator called "as sweet a little fairy as ever fluttered in crinoline over a green sward or sunny slope." A grand prize, for best all-around performance, was a belt with "Champion" on it in gold letters, and a massive silver buckle engraved with crossed skis. News reports, however, failed to name the champion.

After that strenuous day, all contestants and more besides trooped over to the Excelsior Hotel for a ball. There, said a correspondent, "the beauty and chivalry of the district tripped it through waltz, quadrille and fancy dance, until roseate morn had fairly dawned from the eastern sky." Perhaps they all scrambled up topside to view the gorgeous sunrise.

To welcome the New Year of 1867, townsmen turned out for a grand parade headed by the Snow Flake Brass and String Band in full uniform: drum major, violinist, guitarist, and gongist. First in line were two marshals, "with drawn corkscrews," then three aids, followed by the speaker of the day, members of the Meadow Lake Board of Brokers and citizens generally. The orator, A. J. Adams, delivered such a moving address, said the *Sun,* "that the Marshals . . . overcome by the pathos of the speaker . . . were quieting their nerves with a bottle of soothing syrup." The celebration wound up with another lively dance at the Excelsior Hotel.

St. Patrick's Day had to be celebrated, too. On the program were a poem, an eloquent oration and once more an all-night ball. "It may surprise your readers," said a correspondent of the Nevada City *Transcript,* "to learn that more than forty ladies were present, and that a majority were dressed as elegantly and fashionably as at any similar scene in a city."

These people were gay and festive. Whether or not the mines ever paid off appeared to be of less moment to them than good-natured enjoyment of good fellowship. Gallant, courageous, and hearty—ski by day and dance till roseate morn—they had a sense of humor that, in the best tradition of mining towns, allowed them to make fun of themselves. Also in the tradition was a robust spirit, so vigorous that it still seems as vital today, as vibrant and alive as it was a hundred years ago.

They did not neglect town affairs or the welfare of the mind. Economy-minded trustees reduced the pay of the town marshal to $5 a month, and opened a free public school on B Street. J. A. Brumsey, teacher, instructed over forty pupils ranging in age from five to fourteen years. The rejuvenated Literary Club met periodically, ladies admited this time. A Miss Wood proffered a recitation, "excellent in articulation and inflection," and the versatile Miss Clara Head sang " 'Tis better to laugh than be sighing" in a manner described as "her usual clear and forcible style." Judge Tilford gave a talk on "Results of the American War." Brumsey read a paper entitled "The Material, Purifying, and Fraternizing Principles of Humanity."

In general, residents faced the austerity of the summit with chins up, but now and then the steady pressure of winter slowed the pulse and depressed the emotions. January had only seventeen days of snow, but one storm that raged for a week left the editor of the *Sun* in a low mood. He expressed his gloomy feelings in verse: "No sun, no moon,/No morn, no night, /No sky, no earthly blue,/No distant-looking view,/No road, no street,/No tother side the way,/. . . No cheerfulness, no healthy ease,/No butterflies,/Nor yet no bees." He went on in prose: "Here we are, and here we have been, cooped up like an old hen with her chickens, for the past seven days. It has snowed and blowed incessantly . . . . The snow has drifted so deep around our office that we could not see the light of day if there was any, but have our doubts as to there being any."

It is not surprising that a long Arctic season of snow and cold bearing down relentlessly and, as it must have seemed, endlessly, sometimes oppressed the spirit. Yet dejection was transitory. Perhaps the prevailing temper was better implied by Miss Eliza Pittsinger. She was not on the scene, but she eulogized from somewhere in the valleys where the temperature was higher. "Meadow Lake!" she wrote, "whose Autumn beauties upon which we so richly feasted are now hidden beneath a heavy mantle of snow. . . . Lovely spot! . . . lying away up there, beneath thy shroud of awful purity! dream away thy winter loveliness, and leap forth to the call of Her who shall redeck thy shivering form with garments gleaming with the rosetints of youth and joyousness!" That was a more suitable way of putting it, more seemly than despond.

The *Sun's* editor, soon in a more cheerful state of mind, hammered away on mining topics. Again stressing the need of capital for developing mines and building mills, he argued for more efficient mill machinery and for more intelligent treatment of the peculiar ores of the region. "Nowhere, within the range of our observation," he said, "can such natural inducements for the investment of capital be found, as in Excelsior." The paper published mining news as it came to hand, although such items were not plentiful, most companies and claim owners doing no work during the hard winter. Among the larger outfits, however, several that had built shelters over shafts were carrying on regardless of weather.

When the California Company struck the main ledge at a depth of ninety feet, its stock jumped from $2 to $15. As soon as the California mill was in running order, said the *Sun*, "there is no doubt that before many weeks, this company will at least weekly, if not daily gratify our eyes with the yellow golden bricks, that go so far to sustain trade and commerce." The U. S. Grant mill, going night and day on rock paying about $60 per ton, did gratify the eyes by producing from one week's run a bar worth $1,200. The Golden Eagle Company, on a ledge said to be "one of the richest gold veins in the State of California," was getting out rock that experts estimated would go $2,500 to the ton. A reporter for the Virginia *Enterprise* said that he had seen "a quantity of excellent looking ore from the Mohawk and Montreal mine . . . four assays of which . . . yielded at the rate of over $65 to the ton. This was considered about average ore, and there is enough of it in sight at the mine to last for many years to come."

Forecasts about the future of the district were less extravagant than they had been the year before, but Meadow Lake adherents were no less assured of ultimate success. The *Sun* came out with a confident statement: "All agree that the mines are here, and that treasures untold lie hidden in the mountains, and that in the course of time this district will be one of the most productive of the precious metals in the State." In the same editorial the editor delivered a strong sermon about apathetic claim owners, "each waiting for another to make a strike that will bring his property up without any effort of his own." Get going, you miners, said the paper, "take your sledges and drills, throw off your coats, and resolve not to wait until somebody prospects for you. . . . go in . . . on your muscle, and take our word for it, money will seek you to share dividends."

As early as the middle of March some began to think of warmer weather ahead. "We now hope," said a rhapsodic correspondent, "that young Spring, whose advent to the summit is welcomed morning and evening by the joyous carol of the birds in our evergreen forests, has at last snatched his icicled sceptre from the hoary old tyrant on the mountains." The hope was delayed of fulfillment for about six weeks, yet by May the deep snow was melting at the rate of some five inches a day. As it flowed off and buildings began to be recognizable, townsmen surveyed the havoc wrought by the great weight of drifts. The Enterprise quartz mill had collapsed, but since it had never been much good, its loss was not calamitous. The Bloody Run theater was a wreck, likewise the Warren House, a hotel completed only a few months before, on which the owner had spent his last cent. A barn or two had gone down, and of one livery stable the only part left standing was the front wall. The town of Mendoza, empty of inhabitants, was crushed to a splintered ruin. Wiseacres said that roofs should have had a steeper pitch to allow snow to slide off, but at those thirty-foot depths where it was supposed to slide to they did not say.

Dedicated believers surmised that the season of 1867 would see a stampede like that of 1866. Some were convinced that the outlook was better than ever. In May, when travel was still not easy, only a little less difficult, arrivals did increase somewhat, occasionally as many as twenty in one day. A spate of favorable mining items had the usual provocative effect. Prospectors discovered a new ledge, called Green Emigrant, which was said to be richer than anything heretofore found in the district. Two local citizens, Jake Ford and Ed Richardson, prepared to build a furnace to reduce sulphurets. The Pine Tree Company was getting out "some splendid looking rock." Shooting Star assays ran from $150 to $680 to the ton.

Nothing equaled a good assay as a means of getting fortune-hunters off the mark. They drifted in to Meadow Lake, though not in the surging numbers of the previous year. The town took on a semblance of life, but it was not crowded or noisy with gold-rush hubbub. Sober-minded residents had no desire to contend with the turmoil of a stampede anyway, with its bummers, loafers, misfits, and general hurly-burly. What was wanted, said the Nevada City *Gazette*, were "sane men, with capital and energy, not lunatics." In late June the *Sun* predicted that within a month 500 men would be employed in the mines.

Trying to arrange a program for the Fourth of July, citizens gathered in one of those confused meetings that were typical of the place. Four elderly gentlemen, fond of hearing themselves talk and full of patriotic sentiments, monopolized the session, each making a long speech on the best way to celebrate the Fourth, and disagreeing loudly with the others. While they were shouting and wrangling among themselves, at great length, the audience one by one quietly stole away. Nothing was accomplished that time; nevertheless, the Fourth was properly observed. A. G. Rollins delivered an oration, J. A. Brumsey read the Declaration of Independence, and fireworks on the lake lighted up the night.

For the first time politics agitated the population with the customary strong opinions and prejudices of party bias. After the Democrats had formed an organization of some ninety members, Union men—Republicans, that is—also got together to support George C. Gorham for Governor. The pro-Union *Sun*, skimping mining topics for a time, plunged in with many editorials endorsing the Union ticket and principles, all in the familiar assertive tradition of small town weeklies everywhere.

At one Union meeting Brumsey, a Democrat, engaged in a sort of debate with A. G. Rollins, Union candidate for the state legislature. "It is unusual," said the *Sun*, "for a Democrat to speak at Union clubs, but the people of Meadow Lake wanted to give the poor fellow a show, well knowing that Democratic principles gain nothing by discussion." Republicans, who considered their party the only true exponent of national union, still suspected Democrats of harboring disunionist Copperhead views.

On election day the town, casting 99 votes, gave Gorham a plurality of sixteen over his Democratic opponent, Haight—but the latter won the governorship. At a time when the political air was hot in Washington, the local contest in the high Sierras generated the usual campaign warmth but apparently no lasting rancor or bitterness. If any pugnacious supporter got his dander up far enough to be on the fight, the story did not get into the papers. The temporary heat of conflict soon cooling down, the skirmish seems to have been something like an entertaining pastime.

Another diversion was invented by boating enthusiasts, who formed the Meadow Lake Yatching [*sic*] Club. The "Yacht" was an old lumber scow, innocent of mast, mainsail or jib, rigged only with four sets of oars. Made of iron, she was a sturdy vessel but so unwieldy that the club practiced every evening to get the hang of the clumsy craft. Then, commanded by a famous Wells Fargo shotgun messenger named Steve Venard, and loaded with voyagers, this eight-oared barge plowed sedately around the lake on pleasure excursions. Winter or summer, these Meadow Lake people enjoyed themselves.

Enlivened by boating, picnicking and, of course, dancing, summer jogged on pleasantly, though it brought no prosperity to miners or to anybody else. Many mining companies were levying on stockholders for assessments, always a bad sign, for it meant that those mines were not earning enough to meet expenses, let alone pay dividends. Trustees had sometime since relinquished direction of town government, and of the company that had undertaken the installation of a water system no more was heard. Money was scarce, business lethargic, nearly everybody hard up.

Impecunious bachelors banded together in small groups to save on the food bill by doing their own cooking, each taking his turn. Such an arrangement was naturally chaotic and untidy. Ladies, obviously not exemplars of the modern woman, were offended by this encroachment upon their domestic prerogatives. The *Sun* reported that some of them, with determination and mops, moved in on one of these bachelor mess halls to redd up the place while the inmates were absent. The cleanup squad found, as expected, "the fire out, the larder empty, the water-bucket and the coffee-pot and everything else all empty, and ruin and confusion . . . but when those chaps returned, strange, most wondrous strange to tell, the coffee-pot was full."

Times were so far from brisk that to observers elsewhere the town appeared to be sliding downhill fast. A jocular reporter on the Virginia *Enterprise* invented a story about a gentleman who came away from Meadow Lake, leaving behind a population consisting of his wife, a man, and a dog. Then, when the man left, said the story, "His wife and a dog now hold the town." The *Sun* snapped back that the man was probably "one of the class of men of which Meadow Lake has been for a long time cursed with—men who have been compelled to leave the place because their *wives* were unable to support them longer, and whose well known bumming propensities had played their credit out.. . . . The prospects of Meadow Lake were never brighter than to-day. We have got rid of a large amount of the 'scum of creation' which the State of Nevada poured in upon us."

In support of the *Sun's* hopeful view, fifteen or more mining companies were active, and claim owners were finally showing a disposition to open ledges in depth, to test the prevailing belief that veins either got richer as they went down or failed entirely. The U. S. Grant Company, incorporated in San Francisco with a capital stock of $320,000, planned a 20-stamp mill. That, together with substantial backing, "will be the means," said the *Sun,* "of placing it at the head of the list of rich gold producing mines of the Pacific Coast." The Mohawk and Montreal, having struck ore that assayed $600 to the ton, produced a gold bar worth $1,100, on display at Collins' store. The future prospects of this company, said the Virginia *Enterprise,* "are very flattering, and it should not be many months before the present income will be increased so as to afford dividends to stockholders." The Gold Run Company was reported to have hit "a very rich streak" from which it was taking out "some splendid ore."

All such items were nourishment for the hopeful. Meadow Lake, having gone through a dormant period, said the *Sun,* "the Spring-time of her life is approaching, and a healthy and prosperous growth must follow. Our mines, such as have been worked, are showing up splendidly." If only, the paper concluded plaintively, somebody could solve the nagging problem of how to separate gold from all the other things it got mixed up with—iron, manganese, copper, cobalt, arsenic, sulphur, nickel, lead—then "our mines will be the richest in the world."

That problem was yet unsolved despite various processes, roasting furnaces, and reduction works. Sulphurets were always evaluated at so much per ton, and the estimate made the statistics look better, but the gold that was in them stayed there. Notwithstanding news of rich ledges, promising rock, and occasional bullion, Meadow Lake in 1867 was as it always had been, a district of expectancy, of splendid yields due sometime in the future but not just now. The delay was wearing down everybody except the most stout-hearted.

Late summer saw the annual departure of residents for the warmer valleys, some of them leaving permanently because they could no longer afford to live at the summit. A Grass Valley editor remarked that, of those who had invested in the mines, "some have already ceased to pay further assessments, concluding, whether wisely or not, to suffer the loss of what has already been paid, than to spend any money without a better show than at present of getting a return."

The season was ending in a somber way that suggested dissolution. A gloomy reinforcement of that implication was the saddest casualty of the year, the death of the Meadow Lake *Sun*. The paper suspended publication in late November, the editor expressing vague hopes of resuming when times were better, but all knew that a revival was unlikely. The *Sun* had made a sterling effort, keeping up its own courage and bolstering that of others, never losing faith in the district, trying to stimulate people to work harder, and presenting its views, on mining especially, with cogency and vigor. The demise was not a happy omen. The paper would probably be missed by the small coterie of never-say-die citizens resolved to struggle once again through snowbound months up there. They numbered this time only about a hundred people.

# 8

### XXXXXXXXXXXX

# Long Road Down
# 1867–74

THE WINTER of 1867–68, beginning early in October, took charge
in its usual forthright manner with biting cold and heavy snows
that did not melt away until the following July. The only satisfactory mode of travel was by Norwegian snowshoes. A new
kind of "pack train" was a solitary Chinese, who carried his
load on two ends of a bamboo pole.

Of the residents of Meadow Lake, old hands at coping with
summit storms, all that can be said is that they survived. Such
news sources as chatty letter-writers, formerly voluble, had
apparently departed, and the *Sun* was in eclipse. Hence, no word
filtered down this season about dancing or skiing or other di-
verting amusements. In April, a brief item said that "The
Meadow Lake denizens are luxuriating under a weight of
twenty feet of snow, and calculate to get a sight of the sun
sometime in the coming May."

After being mauled by three Sierra winters, the town
showed signs of wear and tear. Months of deep snow, of freezing
and thawing, treated hurriedly-built structures so roughly that
they were becoming down-at-heel. Some deserted houses,
boarded up, had the rejected look of old furniture tossed into
the discard. Others had the rakehelly morning-after appearance
of a tippler not yet sobered up: siding loose, doors hanging

askew, paint worn off, roofs falling apart. A weatherbeaten front, gray and rickety, was replacing the bright facade that had impressed visitors when the town was new.

Appearance suffered further by a catastrophe that destroyed a landmark in late June, 1868. Fire, supposedly started by an incendiary, swept the Lake House, once a center of sociability but now empty of tenants and without a caretaker. The blaze also burned the adjoining cigar store of Henry Reilinger and damaged two other houses. No new buildings went up there. The property in the center of town, corner of Second and B Streets, remained an unsightly blackened mass of debris.

Townsmen, who took such accidents in their stride, were not cast down. They welcomed the return of a few former residents and the arrival of a small number of newcomers who trickled in to give the place an appearance of life. The Excelsior Hotel was in business, and a man named Sheuster was dreamer enough to open a new hostelry. A correspondent totted up other assets: "two restaurants, four stores, six saloons, a post office, two breweries and a milkman. The population consists of about one hundred and fifty men, women and children, three horses, four cows, four dozen chickens, forty dogs, one pig, and a Chinaman."

Meadow Lake did not throb with the driving energy of a dynamic metropolis—"not much more than a one-horse village," one observer said—but devoted followers were undismayed. Friedman, postmaster and old settler of three years' standing, asserted that "This place at present presents a more prosperous and promising appearance than ever before. . . . I intend stopping three years longer, and am quite sure that I will come out with more coin than those who have wandered away and are running from place to place." A correspondent maintained that "The prospects of the District were never better, even in the days of greatest excitement, and the miners are confident that it will prove a fine quartz region."

Perhaps optimists rested their belief on plentiful mining news, which seemed convincing evidence of economic well-being, or at least of a convalescent economy on the verge of becoming healthy. Half a dozen companies or more had kept going all winter, the Empire, down forty feet, working on "fine looking rock," the Enterprise packing in fire brick to line roasting furnaces. The Green Emigrant Company was crushing "first rate rock," and the Lake Company struck a ledge that assayed $349 to the ton in gold. U. S. Grant, Independence, and Kentucky were all blasting away on promising locations. In late summer the Gold Hill *News* reported that a piece of Meadow Lake ore half the size of a walnut assayed $93,770.97 to the ton. That one was surely the assay to end all assays, yet strangely enough it did not set off a stampede of gold-hunters.

The Mohawk and Montreal leaped into prominence. This company had several hundred tons of ore out, a mill under construction on the shore of Phoenix Lake. In mining country papers, story after story about the M. and M. mentioned "a fine body of decomposed free gold," "a deposit of exceedingly rich ore," "first-rate returns," "assays of $32 to $682 to the ton," "rock of exceeding richness," and so on. The mine produced a gold bar of 221 ounces, valued at $3,524.49, which was displayed in the show window of Frederick's jewelry store in Virginia. "The many stockholders in this city," said the Virginia *Enterprise*, "who have held on to their shares through all the trouble and expense of opening the mine and erecting a mill, will doubtless desire to see their first brick."

Unquestionably they did so desire. A gold bar was like an accolade, a citation for meritorious service. More than that, it was solid evidence of income that was essential if finances were ever to get out of the red. None of these Meadow Lake mining companies was a profit-making, dividend-earning concern; all had far more liabilities than assets. Hence, a gold brick was a great morale-builder that lifted the drooping spirits of stockholders who had been paying assessment after assessment and wondering whether their mines would ever, as they put it, "come out."

When the Mohawk and Montreal mill began running around the clock, one week's cleanup yielded $10,000. M. and M. stock went up, the forty employees buying all that was on the market, and the company, as befitted a rising organization, established a head office in San Francisco. "The last assessment was paid promptly," said the Nevada City *Transcript,* "and the Trustees are confident that the result from the ore will pay current expenses and extinguish the debt."

As always, however, stubborn sulphurets went down the drain with tailings without yielding more than a fraction of their gold, and carrying with them a good deal of quicksilver. What to do about it was the ever-baffling question. A new method, called the Hagen superheated steam process, looked experimentally as if it would recover much of the gold and reduce loss of quicksilver. "It is probable," said a California editor, "that the sulphuret problem is now solved." Unfortunately, it was not solved. The Hagen process evidently did not work, for it soon faded from view, to be replaced by a chlorination process. Tests had shown that sulphurets, yielding only about $8 per ton by ordinary milling, returned some $200 by chlorination. The Mohawk and Montreal levied another assessment to put in furnaces and machinery for treating ores by that method, which for two or three months appeared to be the right answer to a vexing problem.

Throughout the spring and summer of 1868 a succession of encouraging mining items created an agreeable impression of fortunes on the upgrade—or rather, in the delayed manner of this district, of fortunes getting ready to begin to rise sometime in the near or distant future. "The mines," said a correspondent, "are said to present a very favorable appearance. . . . We always had faith in the mines, and deplored the lack of capital to push work ahead."

In the town of Meadow Lake steadfast faith nurtured great expectations, but no revival of business occurred, nor any flood of immigration. A good many gay-spirited residents must have left the place, as well as articulate and observant letter-writers, for no news stories tell of boating or picnicking in the summer of 1868. It is impossible to believe that people up there became glum and joyless, yet reporters were perhaps too much concerned with golden promise, rich rock, assays, and depths of mine shafts to chronicle ordinary day-by-day commonplaces that give the historian a revealing view of human beings.

By late December the town was in critical condition, down and not far from out. A hotel that had cost $6,000 was sold for $75, the buyer paying that price for its doors and windows, which he at once carted off. Meadow Lake, said a correspondent, "is now about ready to shuffle off its immortal coil, and is hereafter to be numbered among the things that were. Only about thirty-five persons, great and small, will attempt to pass the winter there. . . . Alas! enchanting meadow, beautiful lake, thy charms are fast passing away, never again, we fear, to return."

He was nearly right. The mortal coil was not yet quite shuffled off, but it was moving toward extinction. When 1869 came in, seven families rattled around among the three hundred or so empty houses, many of which had been crushed by snow. In some of those still standing, interior equipment left intact as if inhabitants had just stepped out for a moment—curtains at windows, chairs, cups and saucers on tables—were pathetic reminders of dwellings once animated by the domestic doings and voices of home. A visitor, passing through, remarked upon "houses with all the necessary furnishings for human habitation, and no sign of man's presence. . . . One sight which struck me as odd, was the presence of a piano forlornly stranded in a bar-room or dance hall." Yet life flickered waveringly, like a guttering candle. The Excelsior Hotel did duty as a public house, one combined store and saloon was open, and a school that had about a dozen pupils. By June, the population had increased to forty or fifty.

Then, in early summer, the exhilarating discovery of a new method of ore treatment aroused everybody. A romantic story about a Mrs. Robert M. Burns said that while she was brooding over the death of a favorite brother, he told her in a dream all the details of a reducing process. These she fortunately remembered and jotted down the next morning. A more prosaic version of the origin was that, while making soap, she noticed the effect of concentrated lye upon heated quartz rocks under her kettle. She imparted her observations, or her dream, to her husband, and thus was born the Burns process, which excited the district for the next three months. After experimentation, Burns was so certain of the worth of the method that he had it patented in San Francisco. One part of the process that riveted attention involved soaking the ore in a chemical solution, of which the formula was a secret known only to the proprietor. There was magic in that mysterious brew.

Burns, together with a man named Blood, leased the old Winton mill for a thorough test of the new process, their efforts assisted, so the papers said, by men of ample capital. Old resident Friedman, who witnessed a tryout of the method, said it was "a decided success." Editors all around hailed what appeared to be the coming of salvation. "People who have examined the working of the process," said the Nevada City *Gazette,* "have confidence amounting almost to certainty, that it will be a success." The Nevada City *Transcript* remarked, with reprehensible lack of gallantry: "Meadow Lake will soon be a prosperous place, and the fact that [the process] was dreamed out and invented by a woman will be no detriment if only it saves gold." The same paper observed a few weeks later: "Since the success of the Burns process is established, the Meadow Lake District is looking up."

The town began looking up, too. Population increased to sixty, "and all able to work," a correspondent said, "are engaged in working the mines." In a fever of anticipation, companies ready to try the new method frantically began to build roasting furnaces, the Mohawk and Montreal planning three of them of 20–25 tons capacity. Eagleson rock, assaying $91.50 to the ton in gold, was to be tested by the Burns process. One fellow re-marked philosophically: "If it does not pay to work for gold it will make first-rate tombstones."

A spurt of action impelled by good auspices made the mid-summer outlook rosy, but by early autumn the bloom had faded. The Burns process did not live up to expectations. It worked on small bodies of ore tested experimentally, but on large quan-tities, secret formula notwithstanding, it was a costly disap-pointment that did not return gold enough for a satisfactory margin over expenses. Almost before Burns disappeared from the news, L. B. Churchill, a Meadow Lake pioneer, announced that, having for a number of years experimented with refractory ores, he had found a process for reducing them. Henry Hartley came up with a process, which the California mill tried on 200 tons of Excelsior rock. James Doling discovered a process that he said broke down the ores without difficulty, and that if he could find the necessary backing he would build a reducing works the following spring.

Mine owners and mills, in a mood of desperation, hysteri-cally seized upon any method that looked useful, yet none of those several processes worked well enough to get gold in paying quantities. Failures caused skeptics to mutter that high assays were probably fraudulent, and that from the start the whole district had been a colossal bilk. Others wondered, out loud, whether Meadow Lake ores were really stubborn or whether they seemed so only because they had nothing to give. One news writer said: "After four years' time and the expenditure of many thousands of dollars, the most tenacious prospector now is satis-fied that there is no gold there."

Sanguine believers could not and would not accept that de-pressing conclusion. Although dashed by setbacks, they did not despair, nor were they willing to concede that this region was not full of hidden wealth. One reporter stated the prevailing view when he said that "those who have been there the longest know that there are many rich ledges in the district, and have faith that a method will yet be discovered of separating the gold at economical rates."

Such a discovery must perforce be postponed to another year. By the beginning of the winter of 1869–70, mining and milling were at a standstill, the town of Meadow Lake more dilapidated. Casual visitors and others helped themselves to doors, windows, furniture, even entire houses, which they packed down to places in valleys below. Some twenty persons who remained at the summit had their choice of residences. Hotels were free for the taking, a number of lodging houses and a good many substantial homes not wrecked by weather or despoiled by cavalier appropriation of property. The devoted remnant of residents, said the Virginia *Enterprise*, "still are firm in the faith that the mines will turn out a big thing for all concerned, although the ores are very intractable. . . . By fire assays, it is known that the gold is there, but the thing is to get it."

Such firm faith should have moved those mountains, but mining affairs remained quiescent during several months uninspired by a new process. The Mohawk and Montreal produced no more gold bars, nor did any other company. None created enough interest to get into the news for some time. Stockholders, instead of receiving dividends, had to settle for expectations based on hope, the while they were dunned for more assessments.

The arrival of summer, 1870, caused a quickening generally characteristic of that season. Several new companies commenced operations, old ones came to life, and a few hardy Meadow Lake veterans returned to prospect and to express the greatest confidence. The U. S. Grant, building a new mill, was said to be "yielding handsomely." The Mohawk and Montreal mill started up. Bull and Culbertson, at Ossaville, were working ledges that "give promise of great richness." A mill at Carlisle was "getting along well." Somebody discovered "some very nice copper ore." The Samarny and the Scoodiac were heard from. San Francisco capitalists were reported to be interested in the district.

All that sort of thing was as familiar as a tale many times told. One of the phenomena of gold country news was the remarkable way fragmentary information, often vague and of dubious reliability, immediately excited the press. A gentleman wandering around in well-tailored clothes was ipso facto a capitalist; a rumor bandied from paper to paper evolved into an established fact. A shaft being sunk, a tunnel run, a new piece of machinery for a quartz mill, an assay, a hint of rich rock somewhere, a mine superintendent with a confident manner and a purposeful gleam in his eye: such items made news stories quiver with heightened emotion.

Repeating an old refrain, the Nevada City *Transcript* said that "The mining prospects are . . . far more encouraging than at any time since Summit City was in full blast. . . . A considerable amount of prospecting is being done, and there is a growing confidence that the miners need only an effective process for the reduction of ores to make them valuable." Despite encouraging prospects, however, nothing of importance happened that summer, and the district dropped from public notice for a year or two.

In 1872 the sole resident of the town was Henry Hartley, who was known thereafter as "The Hermit of Meadow Lake," and who had as companions hundreds of peacefully grazing horses, cattle, and sheep. Travelers told melancholy tales of streets and buildings empty and silent. Gone were the dancers, the thoughtful men discussing ponderous questions at the Lake House, the long-distance talkers who droned on and on at meetings, the gentlemen toasting each other in Napoleon champagne at the Magnolia or the Bank Exchange. Where now were Carl York and his band, where the noisy and convivial fellows crowding in for Ho Joe at Waugamann's bit-house or the Gem, where the rotund hurdy girls?

In the untenanted town, timbers of crushed houses lay awash on the shore of the lake. In front of business houses signs creaked dismally as they swung in the wind: the neatly lettered

name of a broker dealing in Meadow Lake stocks and other first-
class securities, a boot hanging over the door of a shoemaker's
shop, the name of Peter Bauer's bakery. At the office of the *Sun*
was a notice, in large type, on a bulletin board: "Briefs and
transcripts executed neatly, promptly, and handsomely, in accordance with the new rules of the Supreme Court, at the most
reasonable rates. Stock books furnished to order."

A man who went in on snowshoes was appalled by the
stillness and the cold loneliness. Not a single human being in
sight, not a human sound falling upon the ear: no shouting
crowd of ski riders on the hills, no whoops of sylph-like girls
racing down with skill and grace. Through the windows of a
hotel opposite the hall of the Board of Brokers he could see
bureaus in place, crockery, pots and pans, clean linen on beds
carefully made. Where vigorous life had once flowed, the ghostly
vacuum was oppressive, more desolate than if a cataclysm had
wiped out the town, leaving no trace of man.

Reflective writers mused upon the meteoric rise and sudden
decline of this short-lived "city" that its hopeful founders had
expected to become a lusty metropolis rivaling Virginia or any
other mining center. Some called Meadow Lake a prime example
of folly; others were more kindly. Said one: "Of all the eloquent
. . . monuments of that 'dead-work' with which California and
Nevada are so thickly strewed—work consecrated with human
toil, human heroism and suffering, on which money, talent, and
dauntless energy were so prodigally expended, and which all
went for nothing—this is the most striking. . . . Two miles away
to the south, the Old Man lifts his granite face, and looks down
with sad and solemn mien on the swift mutations of human
fortune."

When a reporter from the San Francisco *Bulletin* visited
Meadow Lake in 1873, he received a warm welcome from Hartley, who said that he was greatly encouraged by seeing the population doubled in so short a time. One other man was also there

off and on. The Hermit remarked, said the *Bulletin* reporter, "that the sight of three persons on the streets at once imparted to them quite a thronged appearance." Hartley was a stayer, a good-humored one besides; having enjoyed a solitary life before the town existed, he easily resumed it now.

The town was dead, or nearly so, and other parts of the district were not very healthy either. Winter snow crushed the Mohawk and Montreal mill into disjointed fragments that fell into Phoenix Lake. Nevertheless, the coming of spring, 1873, made mining also come to life. Oscar Maltman, of Nevada City, arrived with equipment for building a chlorination works to operate by a method different from that tried a few years before. He planned to put up his plant near the U. S. Grant, which had its mill going and 500 tons of sulphurets ready to work on. Claiming to have no difficulty in subduing these ores, Maltman "feels quite confident," said the *Bulletin* man, "that he can conquer the obstacle that has so long stood in the way of success here."

As usual, people drifted into the region during the summer, some intent on mining, some to spend a pleasant vacation camping out in the high Sierras. "But, with all its summer beauties and delights," said the Virginia *Enterprise*, "few old Meadow Lakers would much care to revisit the place where they saw their bottom dollar go up the flume. It is only necessary to mention . . . some of the leading claims of that region to give our old-timers the blues for at least six hours."

Yet hard feelings about the district and disillusion over the failure of all processes so far did not vitiate the hope, which soon became conviction, that Maltman's chlorination works offered the true solution to a knotty problem. The Crown Prince Company was said to have "a considerable amount of good ore on hand," and the Kentucky, tapping the ledge at a depth of 100 feet, hit "a fine body of ore." Even the Mohawk and Montreal, surviving the loss of its mill, somehow resumed work. Let us believe, said a reporter, "that a better day will soon dawn upon

[Meadow Lake], re-peopling its deserted tenements . . . and that the mines here, the master impediment being removed, will return the capital and labor spent upon them a fair reward."

The possibility of resuscitating the town met a sharp check. One morning in late September, 1873, fire broke out in the Excelsior Hotel. Attacking in a dry season and fanned by a good wind, the blaze spread rapidly without hindrance from anybody. In a short time it reduced to a charred ruin some thirty or forty buildings in the center of the one-time business section, even part of Smith's fireproof stone building going down. "Thus," said a correspondent, "Meadow Lake has been rubbed out. What with its costly structures and its iron—not a color of gold—mines, many fortunes have been 'planted,' and many men made wretchedly poor."

The town was not rubbed out, but it was badly damaged, the heart of it destroyed. Hartley's house escaped the flames, and a good many other houses remained standing to form a nucleus for restoration if occasion should arise. Of inhabitants besides the Hermit, one family, having laid in supplies enough for six months, remained there during the winter of 1873–74, snow thirty feet deep.

Maltman carried on, forming a company, readying his roasting furnace, working in the district during 1874 and part of the following year. His operations, however, were evidently not satisfactory, for no news stories publicized results, no editorial hurrahs acclaimed the great success of his method. Chlorination, like other processes before it, ceased to attract attention, and the district lapsed into a coma.

# 9

## Indian Summer
## 1875–80

In 1875 the Meadow Lake district was officially ten years old. The anniversary brought forth no birthday tributes or bouquets, but some papers published reminiscences and capsule histories. In these memoirs, disaffection vied with nostalgia. Reminiscers condemned the short-sighted mistake of building an expensive town and costly stamp mills before the mines had been opened, yet fondly recalled the short heyday of that town when it was uproarious and gay.

Ten years was a ripe age, even venerable, for a mining region. More than a few California camps and diggings had gone down in much less time. Disgusted people who had been badly singed at Meadow Lake believed that it, too, was played out, gone up, and a humbug besides. Those who had come away from there broke had little desire to wish the place many happy returns. To the abortive development of the district, "Virginia City," said the *Enterprise*, "contributed tens of thousands of dollars. Hence, there is no music in the name of Meadow Lake to many of our citizens." When the town was ravaged by fire, one reporter said that the rubble of destruction "would please the worst sold Meadow Laker that has been accustomed for years to d—— the day he ever saw the place."

Since the days of '49, adventurers who had hustled off on

one gold rush after another had spent a good deal of time damning localities, from Fraser River to White Pine, which they had struggled over frozen trails and parched deserts to get into. This summit country had conformed to a stereotyped pattern: discovery of gold, followed by an incoming stampede, spurred by hope of large gains, then by disappointment and stampede out. Meadow Lake had gone through that in-and-out experience, but it had not been fatal. Several times consigned to the shelf as done for, the district continued to attract attention. Despite repeated unsuccessful attempts to make the mines pay, regardless of ineffective processes, of large investments far outweighing slim returns, and all the maledictions heaped upon the place, it was still in the public eye.

Soon after the beginning of the year, word of two ore processes, warranted to work and guaranteed cheap, alerted mining country papers, which forecast a stirring revival in the high Sierras. Various parties were reported to be setting out from Virginia and elsewhere for the summit, others to be waiting impatiently for better traveling weather before starting themselves. News stories asserted that extensive mining operations were due to get under way up there when the snow was gone. "It may be," said the Grass Valley *Union,* ". . . that the city of Meadow Lake will soon swarm, as of yore, with an active and excited population, and that the houses after long abandonment will be refitted. Even that famous city's Board of Brokers may be reestablished."

Possibly that last remark was tongue-in-cheek. Nobody had envisaged restoration of brokers, but newsmen's imaginations leaped ahead in breathless stories that aggravated gold fever once more. By spring the temperature had climbed. It did not reach the hysterical point of 1865, but symptoms were similar as emotional editors foresaw another rush. Prospectors were said to be staking off many new locations and relocations, rummaging around among old mines where tunnels were decayed, shafts full of water. Reports said that entrepreneurs claimed timber rights, that one company laid off a new town, unnamed, and that the U. S. Grant was tooling up for a busy season. Lee Butt had a saddle train of sixteen horses running to and from Cisco. William Campbell inaugurated a tri-weekly stage line to and from Truckee.

A company was said to have relocated the town site and to be selling lots, some former owners buying their property over again. Carpenters were called for to restore falling-down houses, also to put up new ones. Haller and Hart refurbished the Cosmopolitan Hotel, and somebody opened an ice cream saloon. (A new look, that one.) "There seems to be but little doubt," said the Truckee *Republican,* "that the past fame of this district will be eclipsed by the fame it will soon gain."

All that newspaper agitation, compounded of a minimum of fact bathed in the romantic moonshine of rumor and fantasy, promised something like a second showing of a ten-year-old picture. Yet the reality, instead of being the expected repeat performance, was only a frail substitute for the original, with fewer extras on the set and much less confusion. By early June, some forty or fifty people had arrived in town, newcomers sifting in irregularly, fifteen per day now and then. No jamming up twenty in a room this time, no boom prices, no rowdy turmoil. Whether refreshments other than ice cream were on tap, correspondents neglected to say. Nobody had to buy a lot, for many empty houses, still in fair condition, could be had for the taking; of that new town supposed to have been laid out, no more was heard.

The crowd was not a seething mob of stampede proportions, but it was select, dignified by San Francisco capitalists and reporters, men with bankrolls from Truckee, Nevada City, and Grass Valley, also from as far away as New York. These gentlemen were unlikely to go howling through town on Ho Joe jags, and they certainly did not intend to ruin their city clothes by splashing around in muddy mine shafts. Henry Hartley, self-appointed reception committee, affably escorted visitors through the town, toured the diggings with them, and displayed the grandeur of the high Sierras like the master of a vast baronial estate. In a sense he was that, having in this district a long-standing vested interest of regard that gave him license to be proprietary. In keeping with that status, he had taken over a larger residence, which he had equipped with the best carpets and furniture he could salvage.

Of the two processes that had caused this influx, one had been discovered by a man named Green. Although reported to be "a most gratifying success," it did not receive much attention because it was soon pushed into the background by a process that seemed more important. This one, invented by Robert M. Fryer, held the stage for over a year.

He was a young man, evidently of some means, who had been a machinist in New York, a harbor engineer, draftsman, and laboratory chemist. In California he began experimenting with stubborn ores, putting up a workshop near the Halfway House between Nevada City and Grass Valley. Here he tested hundreds of samples, carrying on his investigations in close-mouthed secrecy. "Mr. Fryer," said the Nevada City *Transcript,* "is no long haired hermit, nor intellectually fatigued . . . professor with great glasses. He is in the early bloom of manhood, only thirty years of age, and would pass anywhere for a bank accountant or an artist enthusiastic in his profession, but who had behind that enthusiasm a good deal of sound sense and close observation."

In his laboratory he evolved a process of ore treatment and constructed an elaborate device for working refractory rock from the summit. After a number of tests he was of the opinion, which he did not publicize at the time, that Meadow Lake ledges were much less rich than they were reputed to be. Yet of the gold they contained, he was convinced that by his method he could recover better than 90%.

Acting on that conviction, he organized the Fryer Noble Metals Mining Company, capital stock $10,000,000, to operate in

the summit district. Within thirty days shares were selling at
$40. Visiting the high Sierras early in June, to be respectfully
received by those gentlemen of means, Fryer planned works
there to test the new process, and soon thereafter went on to
Washington for a patent, then to New York to interest men with
money.

Traveling around the country and enlisting the support of
eastern investors were moves impressive enough to make Fryer
a man of some distinction. When he went to San Francisco to
contract for heavy machinery, he was received like a visiting
nabob. Stopping for a week at the Occidental, he was dined and
wined and made much of, his hotel room crowded every day
with mine owners and capitalists. By mid-July carpenters were
putting up his Meadow Lake ore-reducing plant, which was
supposed to be in running order in two or three months.

A jubilant press hailed the prospect of "gold by the ton
and population without limit [that] are to follow this new
Aladdin," and confidently asserted that the district would soon
be "the biggest thing out." Meadow Lake, said one editor, "will
very shortly be a place of importance. There is scarcely room
for a doubt on that point." Mr. Fryer, said another, "assures us
that there is no such word as fail in the matter of his enlarged
plant for treating ores by the new process." News of what was
going on up there traveled across the country to the eastern
seaboard. "The miners of the coast," said the New York *Herald,*
"have almost gone crazy over the recent discovery of a simple
means of reducing refractory ores. . . . The discovery is greater
than a dozen Comstock bonanzas."

Fryer was the man of the hour, his prestige enhanced not
only by a strong company with ample backing, but also by
secrecy that had a mesmerizing effect. Though pressed for details about his process, he did not reveal them until his patent
was assured well along in the next year. The Virginia *Enterprise,*
not disposed to be respectful of anybody, complained about this
reticence. "We obtained the impression," said the paper, "that

the Fryer process was so simple that it did not require complicated and expensive machinery; but if five foundries are needed to produce the machinery to set the preliminary works going, we will not say another word . . . not until we get a patent for an iron mine somewhere. . . . We conclude . . . that Mr. Fryer's process is something like the system by which the heavenly bodies are kept in their spheres. The principle is very simple, but it takes all creation to set the thing going."

Meanwhile the town of Meadow Lake, no hive of humming industry, was rather dreary. Capitalists and San Francisco reporters having gone back to counting houses and news rooms, some twenty or thirty quondam residents lived in those broken-down houses, repairing a little here and there but not enough to freshen up the place very much. Jumpers seized eligible lots, but much good that did them, for nobody was likely to buy real estate here. No companies or claim owners were energetically blasting or getting out rock. The Mohawk and Montreal, U. S. Grant and others, going strong a year or so earlier, were not doing enough work to make news. All seemed to be waiting for Fryer's process to produce, but his unfinished plant looked as though it would not be completed until late in the season.

How Meadow Lake people amused themselves, what their pastimes were, if any, no correspondent saw fit to mention. Not a word about dancing, boating, or somebody playing a piano left behind in one of those abandoned bars. Perhaps reporters were too much bemused by golden prosperity just around the corner to give heed to mere social doings. On the whole the town, a dull place during the summer of 1875, did not look or act as if it were on the upsurge.

By early autumn the Fryer boom was still on, despite more growling over his firm refusal to explain his method. When the editors of the Nevada City *Transcript* and Grass Valley *Union,* escorted by the inventor himself, inspected the testing laboratory between the two towns, the visitors described what they saw in long news stories, and wrote editorials expressing faith and confidence. The derisive North San Juan *Times* sniffed that the process must be good because those editors said it was. "Both of them," said the paper, "have seen the machinery and both of them being machinists . . . pronounce the Fryer machinery perfect. . . . That the Fryer process is a success is now placed beyond any doubt." The Truckee *Tribune* was annoyed, too. "Everybody," said the editor sarcastically, "that pretends to know anything about . . . any particular test seems to be pledged to secrecy, but assures everybody else that 'There's a good time coming.'"

That sort of irritation did not lessen general optimism, nor did more serious criticism. Technical publications, such as the *Mining and Engineering Journal* and the *Mining and Railway Register,* said that the Fryer method was merely an imitation of an old process, unsuccessful and long since discarded. California editors leaped to his defense, likewise writers-to-the-editor like "Fair Play," and Fryer himself, all of them engaging in a spirited argument that bantered pros and cons for several weeks. The Nevada *Transcript,* one of his warmest admirers, said that within a year "these carping critics and old smarties who have so much to say in derogation of everyone, will be claiming that they were the firmest friends of the inventor, and knew it was a big thing from the start."

When Fryer's Meadow Lake reduction plant finally started up, late in the season, crushing 24 tons of rock every 24 hours, there was talk of public recognition of his services. A modest man who did not seek the limelight, he begged off. At some future time, he said, "when all my esteemed associates of the East are with me, a repetition . . . of those quiet hospitalities, a dinner in the woods, so frequently extended to me . . . here, will be as truly and heartily appreciated as any demonstration which could be tendered me now."

For some months good fortune seemed imminent as he rode the crest of popularity. Then, about the middle of 1876, the name of Fryer disappeared from the papers. That was a sure sign that something damaging had happened. As one historian tells the story, Independence Day of that Centennial year was selected for a public demonstration of the process. It was to be a big occasion of orators and many spectators, all shielded by a canvas canopy stretched over a full block of one of the streets of Meadow Lake. According to this historian, the spectacle turned out to be a miserable failure, for wagon loads of ore yielded only microscopic returns.

That account may be apocryphal, yet a disaster undoubtedly occurred to destroy confidence almost overnight. Fryer himself said later that after being badly burned about the face he had to give up active management for awhile. During his absence, he said, the works were incompetently run, and while he was convalescing he was pushed out of control by his esteemed eastern friends. He maintained that Meadow Lake ore had had a fair trial, but "the richness of the rock did not in any manner reach the figures I have seen it estimated at by some others." His method probably did exactly what he claimed by recovering nearly all of the gold, but the quantity was not large enough for his associates. They wanted larger profits, more than the ledges had in them to give.

The general public, unaware of backstage corporation power maneuvers, could see only that one more process was getting but feeble returns out of ore that assayed up into the hundreds and thousands of dollars. Those who had heartily praised Fryer now began, with like vehemence, to abuse him. He immediately severed all ties with the Noble Metals Mining Company, began individual experimentation in other mining districts, and turned his inventive mind to new projects, one of them the designing of a steel three-wheeled ocean-going steamship for which he received a patent a few years later.

Only about a dozen people stayed through the summer of 1876 at Meadow Lake. Some of them snowshoed over the Fordyce dam on the Fourth of July, but none of them did any more mining than the law required to keep claim titles intact.

Into the vacancy created by Fryer's sudden fall from favor moved several other aspirants for the role of wonder-worker. Messrs. Knox and Osborne, old hands at running quicksilver works, bought a mill site for a furnace that, said a reporter, "they feel confident will reduce Meadow Lake ores."

A statement like that was good enough to heat up the imagination. A gentleman who visited Virginia, observed the *Enterprise*, "represents things as advancing toward prosperity in that section, and declares his full faith that it will yet become one of the first bullion-producing sections of the State." For ten years Meadow Lake had been in a condition of becoming, no jam today but unquestionably jam tomorrow. Probably no other mining district had ever been nourished for so long a time on little else but hope.

In 1877 the Pittsburgh Company got down to rock that assayed $250 to $450 per ton. The figures caused a slight flareup of excitement that prompted the return of several once-disgusted former residents. A Mr. Crail arrived with a patent on smelting works that he firmly believed would make the ledges pay well. A Professor Crosby had a process that he confidently asserted would get all the gold there was to get. J. A. Gleason, an inhabitant of Meadow Lake, discovered a process that he knew would be "entirely successful."

Observing the parade of processors, coming and going more swiftly than seasons of the year, the Grass Valley *Union* wryly remarked: "We hate to think it, and we hate still more to speak it, but we cannot help at times from thinking it, that maybe there is not so confounded much gold in that Meadow Lake ore as has been imagined. If the fear . . . has any foundation in truth of course no process in the world . . . will get the blood out of the turnip." That view was sensible and probably accurate, but not many people could possibly allow themselves to believe that this district was only a turnip.

In 1878 somebody evolved improvements on the Fryer process, and the Schiveley brothers built a furnace, which unfortunately went to pieces under high heat, but they did better on their second try. Z. A. Willard had a process and a furnace that, it was said, "does the work to perfection." Mr. Harris started a furnace in Maltman's old chlorination works, but when he had been operating only about a month his mill burned down.

Among a profusion of stories about methods and discoverers, all scurrying around among multiple furnaces, precisely who did what is far from clear, but one of them succeeded in producing a gold bar from a ton of rock. The brick was a puny specimen, worth only $35, but it set off loud editorial hosannahs. "Gold! Gold!! Gold!!!" screamed the Truckee *Republican*. Old Meadow Lakers, said the paper, "wandered wildly about the streets in search of crucibles, and mortars, to test therewith the abandoned ore, which now can be successfully worked." Other comments were equally ecstatic: "Meadow Lake is a success!" "With the certainty of working the ores comes the certainty of vast fortunes." "A grand rush to the new mines or to the old ones newly valuable has already commenced," and so forth.

Truckee men formed the Meadow Lake Mill and Mining Company, all the prominent citizens there buying stock for purchasing six thousand dollars' worth of machinery; a hundred Virginia miners were reported to be going up to the summit. When the Schiveley brothers turned out a gold bar worth $300, it aggravated delirium and increased lavish expenditures for mill sites, furnaces and the like, gentlemen with ready cash recklessly throwing their money around with carefree unconcern for cool appraisal. There was a great hubbub over shipping machinery and supplies, several mining companies stocking up on wood and provisions to see them through the winter.

The shaft at the Pittsburgh, said a reporter, "discloses richer and less refractory ore at each foot of descent." At one mine of the Excelsior, working two shifts, he went on, "it is estimated that there are one million tons of ore-producing quartz above a depth of one hundred feet from the surface." Truckee citizens who visited the district were so well pleased that they were ready to invest $200,000 in mines there. They predicted "an unprecedented excitement next Spring."

That prediction, intoned many times over the years, testified to tenacity, to faith and the strength of an illusion that in retrospect seem incredible. Yet these states of mind, or emotion, which existed in men hard-headed and shrewd as well as in men soft-headed and foolish, remained powerful notwithstanding ensuing events that time and again had not borne out the promising forecast. Nor did events in the spring of 1879. No stampede occurred then, no excitement, as various processors faded from view. Knox, Osborne, Crail, Crosby, Schiveley, Willard, Gleason, Harris and no doubt others, unsung and unidentified: all fell into limbo. The continual parade of trial-and-error was farcical but it was pathetic, too, in its buildup of great expectations that were invariably cast down. Truly Meadow Lake was, as one commentator remarked, "the bone yard of processes."

During a trancelike spell of several months, while heavy investors added up their losses, nobody announced a new method for treating this ore. Then, in late summer, James Gould perfected a reverberatory roasting process that produced a gold bar worth $600 from six tons of rock. Approval was prompt and, as usual, fervent. "At Last!" said the Truckee *Republican,* which relished the exclamatory. ". . . Meadow Lake is promised a grand 'come out' again." Gould's success, said the Grass Valley *Union,* was good reason for thinking that "Meadow Lake will yet become a great bullion producing district, equal at least to any in the country." Before long, said a correspondent, "we doubt not, the abandoned mines of Meadow Lake will swarm with busy laborers."

Gould and his associates were full of confidence. As 1880 came on, they said that the only thing needed to make the place hum was plenty of capital for mines and mills. To prove it, they displayed rock that assayed $2,000 to the ton. The revived U. S.

Grant, planning to build a new mill to replace one crushed by snow, intended to get out ore as soon as weather permitted. The ledges of that location were said to have enough in them to keep five thousand stamps going. New outfits like Meadow Lake Consolidated and the Gazelle got busy. Cisco Consolidated, incorporated in New York with a capital stock of $10,000,000, controlled eight claims on which assays ran from $290 to $690 to the ton.

In the air was talk of new machinery coming in, likewise customary rumors of capitalists on the verge of loosening purse strings. "Those who have held on to their locations in Meadow Lake through all its 'ups' and 'downs,'" said the Truckee *Republican,* "are now more than ever confident that they have a good thing. There is going to be a revival in the mining interest there this summer." Even the state mineralogist considered sending a man up to the summit to make an official report.

Thus the summer passed agreeably, enlivened by anticipation and news of great success. Henry Hartley, one of the most steadfast adherents of the district, was "just as enthusiastic as ever," a reporter said, "and firmly believes that section will ere long be the great mining center of the Sierras." Undisturbed by the rise and fall of many processes, he had for almost twenty years used his own methods, working rock by hand, making a comfortable living if not something more than that. Reported to have bonded four mines to Virginia men for $8,000, Hartley, a canny fellow unlikely to plunge rashly, was himself on the way to becoming a minor capitalist.

Otherwise, however, no gratifying production of gold rewarded strenuous efforts, and Gould, like others before him, retreated into obscurity. The New York *Daily Graphic,* noting a "swarm of so-called 'processes'" that "appear every day and drop out of sight at night," remarked that "Nearly all processes will work in the laboratory . . . but, somehow, these process people have always encountered difficulties in actual work that have prevented their scheme from working on a large scale." A better reason for apparent failures at Meadow Lake was that below the rich decomposed surface rock, which always assayed in enticing figures, ledges either pinched out or yielded small returns. The gold, except in occasional pockets, was not there in large quantities.

By the end of the year 1880 reaction had set in once more, and the district was falling into a state of ruin. In a grove of pines Fryer's reduction plant, doors and windows removed, chimney gone, was a lonely shell, prey of the wind and snow. Processors' furnaces were abandoned, hoisting machinery and other appliances were rusting out, timbers going down.

The town of Meadow Lake was in sad condition, every winter having taken its toll by crushing a few more buildings. Grass-grown streets were thoroughfares for squirrels, board sidewalks broken and rotted, and of the Plaza only the barest trace remained. On the porch of many a house a small heap of quartz symbolized somebody's high hopes. Inhabiting the place, said a correspondent, were "ten men, two women, two cats, a dog (dying) and a mule, who occasionally amuses himself kicking down a row of buildings. He kicks down one building at the end and the rest fall as a matter of course." A groundhog wandering in or a bear nosing around, he said, "relieves the monotony considerably. To visit such a spot reminds one of Hood's poem, 'The Haunted House.' "

# 10

### XXXXXXXXXXX

# Hope Deferred
# 1881–92

No ROUSING FORCE less compelling than Gabriel's trump seemed likely to resurrect Meadow Lake, but persistent human efforts labored hard to bring it back to life. Clinicians, diagnosing and prescribing, hovered over the comatose patient like a medical corps with stethoscopes. In the news with surprising frequency during the 1880's, the place was periodically pronounced to be on the verge of a return to consciousness and health. Inventors of processes were less numerous than heretofore, but they were equally positive that they had solved all problems; eager believers, as hopeful as ever, continued to inform the public that the district was a big thing.

If that performance appears extraordinary in the light of a long succession of past reverses, a partial explanation is a constantly changing cast of characters. Of the original Meadow Lakers who had rushed up there in '65 and '66, only a few were around, and of those even fewer were much interested in anything that happened at the summit. Many were far away or they were too disillusioned to care or they had died. But plenty of replacements, who had to find out for themselves, continually stepped in. Taking up the torch, they carried it with the same indestructible enthusiasm, animated by resolute belief in good times coming. Mine ownerships changed hands, and when old companies fagged out or went broke, new ones appeared on the scene, all stimulated by the familiar expectation of handsome rewards certain to come within a few years.

In the autumn of 1881 a reporter said that Meadow Lake mines, "which have been lingering along for so many years, may yet become a source of permanent prosperity to many hundreds of miners. The old town on the lake may one day be rebuilt, and may yet far exceed in glory all that it was in its pristine days." At Carlisle, two mills were running on rock that yielded $70 per ton; Cisco Consolidated was about to start another mill, manned by a full complement of hands—six men, as it turned out. The Truckee *Republican,* a good friend of the district, carried encouraging words: "The predictions so often indulged in that Meadow Lake was 'gone in' do not seem to prove true. . . . the prospects are favorable for quite a lively mining camp in that region in . . . a year or two."

The hero this time was Walter Hamilton, a mining expert of New York and Oakland, who had a brand new process. He found out that gold alone would not melt short of 2,000° F, but that when dipped in melted lead it dissolved at 640°. Then all he had to do was to get the gold out of the lead. Mining authorities claimed that "the most refractory ores can be reduced by this process." Papers, once again printing stock comments, chorused that a successful reducing method was sure to mean a great revival up there, the rise of Meadow Lake as one of the best mining regions of the Pacific coast, wealth abounding for everybody.

Hamilton's success must have been marred by flaws somewhere along the line, for he disappeared as abruptly as he had emerged. Nevertheless, in the early spring of 1882 a man named Lee Butts, of Truckee, evidently thought that business was about to improve at the summit, for he planned to open a hotel and general supply store at Meadow Lake. The Virginia *Enterprise* envisaged a big boom in that camp—if only, that is, somebody stumbled upon the right process.

A company at Burlington, Iowa, sent for a ton of Meadow Lake ore for testing by a method invented by A. T. Hay, a steel manufacturer—just the man, some believed, to wrestle with the stubborn iron in those ores. Of his process the Truckee *Republican* remarked: "They say there is no mistake about its working satisfactorily." Apparently there was a mistake, for no results of the test appeared in the papers, and Hay dropped out of sight more swiftly than Hamilton.

Minor flurries did not revive anything, but neither did they sour the note of cheer. The Virginia *Enterprise,* usually skeptical, maintained that "In the course of time Meadow Lake may turn out to be a first class mining town. The number of men who are able to make mining pay in that region of rebellious ores is constantly increasing." Perhaps, but the number was small and the pay was modest. By summer only two men were at work: Hartley, carrying on as usual at the Pittsburgh, and a Mr. Cromb at the Sunny South.

Later, when a Philadelphia man acquired an interest in several mines, he announced great schemes for hiring a large force and bringing in improved machinery. Good intentions involving new machinery were always satisfying as evidence of confidence, as tokens of determined effort that would surely achieve profitable results. The press delighted to publicize expansive plans, but seldom followed through to find out whether they were ever carried out.

Not many were making mining pay in 1882, nor did anything of note occur the following year. The town of Meadow Lake became more decrepit, nature taking over and gradually restoring a Sierra solitude that was again a haven for deer, quail, grouse and woodchucks, which had been frightened away by the intrusion of man. Some thirty or forty buildings still stood, more or less intact. Empty houses gave transient shelter to a few roving cattle herders and summer campers.

A correspondent rambling around up there found about a dozen miners holding on, doing no more than scratching out a living but still hopeful. One of them, an aging veteran, inquired about mining affairs in the opulent gold regions of Grass Valley and Nevada City. "When you have given him a full account of them and their riches," wrote the visitor, "he will remain silent for a moment, but afterwards brighten up and reply: 'Ah, but wait until we can work these; they are richer than any down there!' "

Faith in the great richness of these ledges was still common in 1884 but unbelievers, more vocal than formerly, broadcast the opinion that processes failed because the metal was not in the rock. As one editor said, "We are a Doubting Thomas." Henry Hartley was not one of the doubters. Stepping forth as an independent operator, he contracted for lumber to build a ten-stamp mill that "by practical experience," said the Truckee *Republican,* "he is satisfied will work the refractory ores satisfactorily." Probably Hartley did make it work, well enough to yield returns that, if not large, were steady and profitable. He was that kind of man.

In late summer a group of eastern capitalists, no doubters either, began experimenting with Meadow Lake ores. They finally hit upon a process that was a combination of several other processes, but their investigations did not come to light until 1886 when, together with others who had been drawn in, they began to build reduction works at the summit to test the rock. On a site near the Excelsior mine, it was to be a costly affair, powered by electricity, crammed with complicated machinery, an assay office attached. Agents of all sorts of financiers were reported to be on the scene. "Last week," said the Reno, Nevada, *Gazette,* "we had represented no less than five companies, one English company, two eastern, one Colorado and one San Francisco."

The complexities of the plant itself were baffling enough, but they were made more so by the piecemeal fashion of putting it together. No top boss superintended construction. Each company having a patent on a crusher or a rotary roaster or some other apparatus, each company agent installed his part of the machinery, then another stepped in, and so on. Harmonious co-ordination was difficult, and finding a manager who understood the whole thing was problematical.

Nevertheless from this plant, "it is confidently expected," said an excited reporter, "the results will be such that all the old-timers who left there in disgust will return and resume work." Others chimed in with the rosy forecasts that had been routine for twenty years. "It is predicted," said the Truckee *Republican*, "that before snow flies there will be a booming little camp where last year there was nothing but a bear [*sic*] plateau on top of the bleakest mountains in the Sierras." "As to the coming year," remarked the Reno *Gazette*, "it seems almost certain now that this will be a lively camp."

Ten men were reported to be employed at the U. S. Grant, twenty at the Excelsior, where a sudden ferment of action ensued. Assays there ran into the hundreds and thousands. "It seems hard to swallow," said a Virginia paper, "yet a gentleman . . . assured a *Chronicle* reporter that the Excelsior mine had more than 1,000 tons of ore on the dump that is 'richer'n mud.' " The Excelsior people put up a telephone line to Cisco and, in expectation of a heavy flow of traffic, began to build a new road to that town.

Such unquenchable optimism deserved a fitting reward, but unfortunately the camp did not boom either before snowfall or after. All those financial and mechanical wizards vanished without a trace. The Excelsior mill broke down after crushing forty tons, from which returns were only $11 per ton. During the next year, 1887, parties reconstructed the works, which ran for a short time in late summer, yielding $10 per ton. That return was not great wealth, but sanguinary followers looked beyond, as usual, to the continually expected golden dawn of some vague tomorrow. A certain Jimmie Hill, displaying Meadow Lake rock that assayed $140 to the ton in gold, $80 in silver, predicted success. "He says," ran a news item, "there is no doubt in his

mind that the day is not far distant when the ores in that district will be successfully and profitably worked." Professor F. L.
Clark, sent up by the San Francisco *Examiner* to inspect the
summit region, announced: "There is no doubt but that Meadow
Lake is a very rich district, and that some time there will be
extensive works erected there which will successfully reduce
the so-called rebellious ores."

One interesting event of 1887 was not widely publicized:
the marriage, in Sierraville, of Henry Hartley and Alice Marion.
London born, she was a widow of twenty-three, younger than he
by thirty years, a painter of some ability, also a competent amateur musician. A reporter described her as "not beautiful but
quite pleasant in appearance, an entertaining conversationalist,
with a fine figure and decidedly English in manner." Having
lived abroad, she seemed more acclimated to city life than to a
lonesome existence in the deserted town of Meadow Lake, but
apparently she accepted the solitude without complaint.

As for Hartley, probably the long-time hermit had crotchets
that made him look like a dubious matrimonial risk, yet as a
steady-going sort of man he was no anti-social oddity or crusty
misogynist. Like Thoreau he undoubtedly was in some ways, but
much more amiable than the uncompromising Concord philosopher who often rasped the sensibilities of his fellow townsmen.
Hartley was not a community irritant, nor was he so set in his
ways that he could not modify them. Rather, his adaptable manner of life implies that he was one of those who, as Montaigne
says, "roll with the rolling of the heavens." If becoming a husband for the first time at age fifty-three meant drastic upheaval
among comfortable bachelor habits, possibly the hermit was
prepared to come to friendly terms with the new dispensation.
To leaven his miscellaneous knowledge gained from reading and
experience, he had the sense of humor that accompanies a flex-
ible nature and that made him, too, a good conversationalist.

He had become a citizen of means, not a bonanza nabob of
great wealth but "well fixed," as the saying went, probably

better off than any other man who had tackled mining in this district. Of all the thousands who had blasted and scrabbled in those granite mountains, very likely he was about the only one who had made a substantial income. He may have held the old-fashioned view that a man should not marry until he could support a wife. Now he could do so with ease. If the bride wanted new rugs, furniture, curtains, chinaware, he could order them from San Francisco or New York or anywhere and pay cash on the nail. No doubt he did just that for, though not a reckless spender, he does not appear to have been close-fisted either.

Where and how this couple met each other, what the attraction was between them, and how they got along up there in the Sierra wilderness are not on record. Since she was more high-spirited than he, perhaps the clash of temperaments in minor domestic crises made sparks fly now and then, as they are likely to do in any marriage, yet no evidence suggests that the match was ill-advised or that the pair were incompatible.

Gold country papers were too much preoccupied with mining affairs to ring wedding bells for the Hartleys. Out of nowhere came news based, naturally, on "reliable authority," of a Baltimore syndicate that planned to build a thirty-stamp mill in the spring of 1888. This organization was said to have engaged an eminent mining specialist and an assayer, one of whom had discovered a process that worked absolutely beyond all question. But no mill went up, no infallible process evolved. The whole thing was so evanescent that it seemed like a mirage glimpsed by an over-imaginative newspaperman.

Next came a discoverer named F. Morris with an economical process he tried at the Excelsior mine. A partial cleanup in midsummer yielded a gold bar valued at $580. An experienced mining expert who observed the operation earnestly declared that the pulpy stuff Morris saved in sluices was worth $5,000 a ton. That sort of thing had the usual stimulating effect. "There is a probability," said one editor, "that in the near future Meadow Lake will be a lively mining camp."

According to the papers, prospectors began arriving at Cisco, via Central Pacific Railroad, in such numbers that a storekeeper there had his hands full outfitting them with supplies. But no remarkable changes occurred at the town of Meadow Lake, no stirring revival of industry, no startling increase of population. The state mineralogist reported that in this district the Excelsior was the only mine on which much work was being done, and that rock there yielded by the Morris method at the rate of $6 per ton. That figure hardly seemed of a size large enough to cause a furore, but since the process was cheap, some canny onlookers evidently believed that the modest return was worth a second look. After all, as one man said shrewdly, if the rock were not superlatively rich, "there is an abundance of it and it promises to exceed in the outcome any mining development on the coast."

The Morris process kept on going into 1889, saving 97% of the gold, even inducing the Comstock Bonanza King, John W. Mackay, to send up two experts to investigate. Other experts from Utah, San Francisco and elsewhere jostled each other for a good view of what was going on at the Excelsior. Prospectors were said to be crowding in "thick and fast," but they must have got lost in the woods somewhere because they did not reach Meadow Lake. A traveler returning from the summit told of finding the town "comparatively deserted, there being only two men and four women in sight. One man, a shoemaker, cobbles up the shoes and boots of passing cowboys and prospectors, and looks out for sundry claims in which he and others are interested. The other man is James [*sic*] Hartley. . . . He is still hopefully waiting for those refractory ledges to give up their wealth." That writer might have been more observant. Merely sitting around hopefully waiting for some miracle-worker to conquer the ledges for him was not Hartley's style at all. He was a do-it-yourself man.

Then Morris disappeared to join the army of all other rejected processors, and those experts presumably reported unfavorably, for no more was heard of them. By the summer of 1890, however, the Nevada City *Transcript* reported that "a number of practical miners of this place who have been operating in that district . . . have great faith in the mines there and are confident that they will ultimately be successfully worked."

A man from Pennsylvania showed up with a vapor process he had invented, tested some 200 samples of Meadow Lake ore, then vanished as if himself vaporized. The slow-but-sure Hartley struck a pocket from which he pounded out over $1,000 in gold, and the Hercules Mining Company announced plans to start a chlorination works. A strong syndicate was reported to be taking over the Excelsior mine with the intention of commencing vigorous operations in the spring. Late in the year a correspondent said that "There will unquestionably be a great amount of work done in this district next season, and if success follows, and it surely will with proper care, the Meadow Lake district will fairly hum with prosperity."

The repetition of that prophecy, an annual pronouncement for twenty-five years, was both amusing and touching. It was whistling in the dark, a brave attempt to deny reality, hoping against hope, an unbelievable display of wish-fulfillment. The end of every year brought forth assurances of splendid events, rich with long-delayed rewards, that were certain to happen next season or possibly the season after that, but they never did happen. Meadow Lake did not hum with prosperity in 1891. Indeed, nothing up there hummed with enough noise to gain the attention of correspondents or editors.

Toward the end of the year Hartley was reported to have bonded one of his mines to parties from Denver for $60,000. In a gesture consistent with that affluence, he sent his wife off on a long tour of England and the continent. "It is understood," said the Truckee *Republican* in November, "that in the spring active operations will be inaugurated and it is not unlikely that the old camp will boom in a few years."

In London in 1892, Mrs. Hartley tried to negotiate the sale to a British syndicate of one of Hartley's mines on the Excelsior ledge for £100,000, but the deal fell through. On October 22 of that year, while she was still abroad, Hartley unexpectedly

Henry H. Hartley.

*California State Library, Sacramento, California.*

died. His widow suspected murder. Later, when she had the body disinterred, he was found to have died of opium poisoning. One of her former suitors seemed a likely poisoner, but no convincing evidence could be found against him. What caused her to suspect murder, who administered the opium and why: these are questions that have remained unanswered.

For Hartley, a mild-mannered, retiring man, not the belligerent sort who incurs murderous animosities, the end was strange and shocking. For Meadow Lake, the loss of its first citizen, its oldest settler, and only permanent resident, made it truly a ghost town.

# 11

## Aftermath 1893–

The winter of 1892-93 was the first in Meadow Lake history during which not a single inhabitant remained at the summit. Not much survived up there to shelter anybody. About twenty structures stood among the ruins of many others, the stonework of Smith and Perkins' costly building still standing as a derelict reminder of once bright aspiration. In the country roundabout were at least eight deserted and rotting stamp mills and several collapsing smelters. Now and then a careless vagrant started a fire that burned down a mill or an old house.

The forest had moved in, trees growing in the middle of roads that had been laboriously grubbed through that rocky and resistant terrain. The town as an entity was finished, its chronicle no longer concerned with human affairs but only with the recording of further dismal stages on the way to the vanishing point. Nevertheless, for more than half a century afterward, historians and mining operations periodically brought into notice the name of Meadow Lake.

Alice Hartley moved to Reno, where she established herself as a drawing teacher, opening a studio in the Bank of Nevada Building. For a time she and a man named Ed Roening attempted to work Hartley's Excelsior claims, but when they could not make a go of it, they leased the property. Shortly thereafter she made headlines in a spectacular way. In July, 1894, she shot M. D. Foley, Nevada state senator and president of the Bank of Nevada—shot him twice.

Indicted for murder by the Grand Jury, she came to trial in September in the District Court of Reno, the sensational circumstances attracting a full complement of newsmen from San Francisco, Virginia, and elsewhere. The evidence was fraught with implications so disturbing to Victorian mores that when Mrs. Hartley took the stand, ladies were barred from the courtroom.

She testified on her relations with Senator Foley, whom she had naturally met as a tenant of the building in which he held forth as bank president. According to her evidence, he was an unscrupulous man. Having attempted to seduce her, she said, he called late one night in January, plied her with brandy until she fainted, then accomplished his fell purpose. Six months later, when she was pregnant, Foley seemed disinclined to assume any responsibility. When he appeared to be concerned only about the effect upon himself of a possible scandal, and even made vague threats, she retaliated with the lethal fury of a woman scorned. It was clear that, though her recourse was violent, she had no doubts that her action was justified.

A good many people agreed. Since the testimony revealed Foley as a typical predatory male and herself as the woman betrayed, public sympathy was mainly on her side. In the West, the routine verdict in such a case was acquittal of the defendant. Nevertheless, the Reno jury brought her in guilty of murder in the second degree. Denied a new trial and sentenced to eleven years, she served two and was then pardoned by the governor.

Thus, in an indirect way, Alice Hartley provided Meadow Lake with an episode more melodramatic than any that had ever occurred up there when the town was at its roaring best. Otherwise, no dramatic events enlivened the summit region during the 1890's or subsequent years. With the passing of time, observers and analysts acquired more detachment and perspective. Looking back after almost thirty years, Dan De Quille remarked sadly that the original rush 'to Meadow Lake was "The most disastrous mining excitement ever participated in by the people of the Comstock." In 1893, Waldemar Lindgren, of the United States Geological Survey, after a reconnaissance of the district, published an adverse report. "Considering the difficulties of access and climate," he said, "there is some doubt as to whether any of the deposits can ever be worked with profit. The ores will not average more than from seven to ten dollars per ton at the most."

Yet still extant were a dwindling number of the dedicated faithful, who were as strongly convinced as ever that unheard-of wealth locked in those ledges needed only the right key to open the strong box. "Some day," said a writer in 1893, "a way of working the ore will be hit upon; then, perhaps, there will be seen on the shores of the lake a new town that will far surpass that which the old pioneers left behind them when the 'iron entered their souls' and they left the country."

Mining went on throughout the decade in a desultory way, once in awhile causing a slight flareup of gold fever in some newsman's imagination. "It is reported," said a paper in January, 1895, "that there will be a great rush to the Meadow Lake district when the snow shall have disappeared." By this time most editors, who knew that a great rush was unlikely, were more diverted than impressed by that refrain. No stampede occurred, of course, when the snow disappeared or at any other season.

The lessees of Hartley's Excelsior claim remodeled the mill, but when they could not make the ore yield profitably, they closed down. In 1895, a company leased the Washington mine on Old Man Mountain, installed a wire cable of 2,650 feet from the summit of the Old Man to their camp at Carlisle, got out several carloads of rock by that expensive method, then had to quit when their lease expired. The next year a Colorado partnership purchased the Oro Fino mine with the intention of developing the property, but nothing of note happened there.

Then B. A. Cardwell appeared with a process that he claimed saved 96% of the gold. He even began to build, again, that road to Cisco in the hope of establishing a daily stage line. Capitalists from San Francisco and Salt Lake City were reported to be mousing around, as often they were said to have done in the past, acquiring claims and negotiating for a smelter. Talk of putting up furnaces and concentrators was noised about.

All such items were familiar but, briefly reported in a matter-of-fact way, they did not make the old fire blaze with its former heat. In 1898, the United States Geological Survey once more dispassionately concluded that "Scattered veins . . . and . . . a vein system of some importance, though not very rich, is found in the vicinity of Meadow Lake and Old Man Mountain." Those who were disinclined to believe that these veins were not very rich ignored that conclusion.

Captain E. O. C. Ord and associates organized the Crystal Lake Gold Mining Company, inspected the lodes and built a ten-stamp mill, also a boarding house at the Excelsior ledge. A partnership of Giffen, Butt, and Gay put up an eight-stamp mill at Carlisle. At the old California mine, Clark and Brown struck a rich pocket from which they took $7,000. This find was said to have stirred up gold-hunters. "Already," ran a news story of early autumn, 1899, "prospectors are beginning to search for the precious metals and no doubt some will be successful, as there is plenty of good float" (gold in particles so small and thin that they float; also called flour gold). If prospectors went in, they did not arrive in numbers large enough to cause over-crowding.

After the turn of the century Meadow Lake as a gold region was still not out of mind. In 1901, the Girard Mining Company, of Sacramento, operated a mill, and an eastern company was reported to be building a rotary roasting furnace, hauling in fuel oil from Truckee, 33 miles away. In 1902, Charles W. Raymond, a mining engineer, maintained that the district did not deserve its unsavory reputation. The veins, he said, were "well defined and important . . . the ores carry gold values and often are high grade." Climate was good, transportation facilities likewise. In short, the region offered "excellent inducements to investors as a profit-paying mining camp. . . . pay ore is present in large quantities, and the extraction of the gold is practicable by ordinary, well known, simple and inexpensive methods." If those statements were true, it is difficult to understand why Meadow Lake had never been a profit-paying camp.

In 1906, Charles M. Schwab, the Pittsburgh steel man, was reported to have offered $60,000 for the holdings of John Clark and $100,000 for the mines and mill of a Mrs. Bonnifield. She held out for $150,000. Agents of the Guggenheims were said to be picking up options on good claims. So ran the stories. How much was fact, how much was embroidered fiction is impossible to say.

No memorable event occurred during 1915, the fiftieth or golden anniversary year, and no celebration. There was no such thing as an organization of old settlers of Meadow Lake or an annual reunion of summit pioneers who had lost their shirts up there. Mining became more fitful as various attempts to exploit veins were generally unsuccessful because of low-grade ores and the absence of much free gold. The state mineralogist, who gave the region a brief glance in his report for 1924, estimated that since 1865 the total bullion yield of the district was about $200,000. That output was a long distance short of the millions that had been expended there.

In 1936, the state mineralogist published a more thorough scrutiny, prepared by A. L. Wisker, a San Francisco mining engineer. He admitted that the ores were not high grade—worth $6 to $10 per ton on the average—but suggested that if a number of claims could be consolidated in an economical large-scale mining operation, it should pay. Nobody saw fit to act on that suggestion.

By the 1940's, nothing remained of the town of Meadow Lake. Faintly visible were the boundaries of the Plaza and dimly the outlines of wide streets lined by fragments of board sidewalks. Not a building stood, not even Smith and Perkins' stone walls, the ruins marked by rusty pieces of metal scattered about and broken timbers in splintered disorder. All over the nearby country were weathered ore dumps and shallow excavations that pockmarked the granite, indicating claims that had once been briefly worked on, then given up. Deeper shafts were full of water, many crumbled by caving. No mining of any consequence had been carried on for twenty years.

In 1958, Wisker again examined the controversial summit country. As if to confirm the troubles of all those processors and other frustrated treasure-hunters, he found these ores very complex. In "this most highly mineralized area of California," as he called it, he isolated 28 elements in samples of Meadow Lake rock. Small wonder that old-fashioned milling methods failed to cope with such a variety. In the light of improved metallurgical techniques, he believed that the district merited a resurvey, provided it was conducted by qualified geologists. "If Meadow Lake measures up to its geological indications," he said, "a smelting operation is essential; and the high capital investment must be protected by an examination unequivocally establishing every pertinent fact essential to success of such an enterprise."

He implied that success was possible, yet so temperate a statement was hardly likely to arouse the kind of enthusiasm that had resulted in heavy spending in years gone by. Whether an expert resurvey was made is not on record, but nobody moved in with faith and machinery, and nobody trumpeted expectations of golden prosperity. After almost a century of periodic excitements, of hopeful promise, of breathless predictions of great wealth, the district ceased to attract attention.

Today the high Sierra country, somewhat like the uninhabited region it was when Henry Hartley arrived at the summit, is a pleasant camping ground for tourists and picnickers. The Hermit of Meadow Lake is still there in a small cemetery shaded by a grove of pines on a hillside.

No ruins remain now to remind the visitor that a bustling town once stood on the lakeshore. The silvery lake is there, the lush meadow, the gray granite ridges dominated by Old Man Mountain but, aside from the sturdy Yuba dam, no stick or stone left by the hand of man. Long gone, too, are all the Ho Joe fellows, the snowshoe girls, the brokers, the eager rock sharps, the sailboat mariners, their hopes no longer of concern to them, or their disappointments. To many who lived up there at the summit, summer and winter, disappointments seemed of less consequence than enjoyment of their own ways of making life agreeable. They did not get much gold, if any, but they accepted the vagaries of fortune with good nature and aplomb. "Nowhere in the mountains," said Dan De Quille, "was there to be found a more beautiful place than Meadow Lake, or a happier people than those who made the town their home."

# Notes

To avoid peppering the text with footnotes, I have grouped them here according to page numbers, which appear in the left margin, followed by initial words of quotations, proper names and so forth.

N.B.   When California papers mentioned "Nevada," they meant Nevada City or Nevada County, California. The Territory and State of Nevada were usually called "Washoe." "Virginia," as used by western papers and as used in this text means Virginia City, Nevada. All newspaper references are to California papers unless otherwise indicated.

## 1. The Big Thing

3 "The Miner's Ten Commandments" / Written and published as a Lettersheet by John S. Hutchings, an Englishman and forty-niner who made and lost several fortunes in the mines, these Commandments were so popular that 97,000 copies were sold in one year. Other commandments direct the miner not to jump anybody's claim, not to gamble, not to steal tools, not to work in the rain, not to get discouraged, and not to commit unsuitable matrimony.

3 "There will be divine service" / "A Miner's Sunday in Coloma" (From the Writer's California Journal, 1849–50.), *Century Magazine,* June, 1891, 260.

3 Mother Lode / A northwest-trending system of veins on the western slope of the Sierra Nevada. About a mile wide and 120 miles long, it extends from Mariposa County to northern El Dorado County. Prospectors, however, explored well beyond those limits.

4 place names / Other place names of California mining country are: Barefoot Diggings, Blanket End, Bloody Run, Bloomer Hill, Blue-Belly Ravine, Bogus Thunder, Bottle Hill, Buster Flat, Centipede Hollow, Chucklehead Diggings, Dad's Gulch, Delirium Tremens, Devil's Basin, Dirty Bar, Dogtown, Donkeyville, Drunkard's Bar, Dry Town, Egg-Nog Settlement, Fair Play, Five-Cent Gulch, Flea Valley, Forlorn Hope, Frytown, Fur-Cap Diggings, Greenhorn Cañon, Groundhog's Glory, Hang-town, Hardscrabble, Hell's Delight, Hen-Roost Camp, Hungry Hollow, Jim Crow Cañon, Louse Village, Lovers' Hollow, Milk Punch Bar, Moonlight Flat, Moonshine, Mountain's Brow, Mugawamp, Murderer's Bar, Nip and Tuck, No-eared Bar, Nut-cake Camp, One Horse Town, Paint-Pot Hill, Pancake Ravine, Pepper Box, Peppermint Hill, Petticoat Slide, Pitchfork, Plug-head Gulch, Poker Flat, Poodletown, Poorman's Creek, Poppet Diggings, Potato Hill, Puke Ravine, Puppytown, Purgation

Ledge, Push-Coach Hill, Quack Hill, Ragged Breeches Bar, Ranty Doodler Bar, Ratrap Slide, Roaring Camp, Rot Gut, Rough and Ready, Rowdy Bar, Rum Blossom Plain, Salt Pork Ridge, Sardine Bar, Seven-by-nine Valley, Seven-up Ravine, Shinbone Peak, Skin-flint, Sky-High Diggings, Slapjack Bar, Slumgullion, Sorefinger, Stud Horse Gulch, Swellhead Diggings, Tin Cup Diggings, Tip Top, Town Talk, Two-Cent Ranch, Whiskey Slide.

"Bar" was not a saloon but a flat on the convex side of a bend in a river. Free gold carried down by the current lodged in these bars, which were often rich, the gold being obtained by panning or sluicing. Camps at such places took their names from the bars.

Within a decade or two after '49, western society, particularly in well-established towns and in cities like San Francisco, had moved beyond the free-and-easy frontier stage into self-conscious propriety that reprehended earthy place names as ungenteel, and some were watered down to make them more respectable. Bedbug became Freezeout, then Ione. Hangtown turned into Placerville, Humbug into North Bloomfield, Mud Flat into El Dorado, Gouge Eye into Pleasant Grove, Pokerville into Plymouth, Delirium Tremens into Omega, Fiddletown into Oleta, Rabbit Creek into La Porte. Cherokee Flat, also known as Forks in the Road, became Altaville.

4 the vigor of youth / Many historians have remarked upon the youthfulness of men in mining camps. See Charles Howard Shinn, *Mining Camps;* also Mark Twain's comments on "bright-eyed, quick-moving, strong-handed giants," in *Roughing It,* chap. LVII, and his description in Notebook #3 (1865) of a 38-year-old six-footer at Angel's Camp: Indian fighter, miner, and an educated man fluent in French and Spanish.

5 "Choose your able-bodied men" / Lettersheet, "Digging Gold," n.d.

5 "feels thoroughly equipped" / *Transcript,* March 30, 1882.

5 rock assaying hundred of dollars / An assay could be, and often was, misleading. Sometimes it was deliberately so when an unscrupulous claim owner selected for assay an obviously rich sample to delude prospective buyers into believing that the whole claim was equally rich. Dishonest mining company officers occasionally cooked dividends by the same process. When a good assay made the stock rise sharply, they declared a divi-

dend, then sold out before the price fell and the fraud was exposed. Mark Twain makes entertaining comments on assays in *Roughing It,* chaps. XXX and XXXVI.

5 "with their blankets upon their backs" / VC *Union,* May 25, 1866.

6 Old Schimmerhorn / *News,* July 12, 1866. Characters were nu-erous in the gold country. San Francisco cherished a corps of eccentrics, the most famous of whom was Joshua Abraham Norton. He proclaimed himself Emperor of the United States and Protector of Mexico, dressed the part in full uniform, and issued edicts from time to time. San Franciscans were very fond of him and his two faithful dogs, Bummer and Lazarus. In Virginia, Captain Jim, Chief of the Washoes, was a great favorite. The VC *Union,* June 18, 1864, reported a visit from a polite mild-man-nered Irishman, who announced himself as Jesus the Savior. A wandering character named John Kelley, known as "Kelley the Fiddler," was said to have been paid $100 a day to play for dances in mining camps. At the end of a year he had no money and owed the bar $38.

7 "They never dispute a bill" / "Bummers," *Gazette,* July 18, 1865. This writer divided bummers into two classes: "the low, de-graded bummer, who sleeps in the street, or under a shed, and begs whisky"; and "the cunning, jolly, professional bummers, with just brains enough to adopt some profession, but too indo-lent to attend to it."

7 "People ought to respect me" / "Soliloquy of a Loafer," GV *Union,* January 3, 1866.

8 had seen the elephant / As defined by Stewart Edward White: "This animal stood symbolically for the whole business of gold seeking. When a San Franciscan told a friend that he'd about decided to 'see the elephant,' he did not mean that he was going on a toot, but that he intended to take a flier at the mines." See "The Elephant as They Saw It." In the Civil War any man who had been under fire was said to have seen the elephant.

8 frozen out / According to mining law, when assessments were levied on mining stock, failure to pay meant relinquishing the stock for sale at auction. Hence, the freezeout technique of financial operators was to levy assessments until the harassed owner could no longer pay, then gather in his stock. This practice was a common tactic on the Comstock.

8 "Northern miners" / *Journal,* March 21, 1860.

8 Insanity / San Francisco *Courier,* n.d., reprinted in *Journal,* September 24, 1851.

9 "situated in" / *Journal,* May 6, 1856.

10 Whatcom House / San Andreas *Independent,* July 10, 1858.

10 "Our Fortune-Hunter" / GV *Union,* July 19, 1866.

10 Dame Shirley / Louise Amelia Knapp Smith was a native of New Jersey. Something of a blue-stocking, she was a relative of Julia Ward Howe, a friend of Emily Dickinson and an admirer of Margaret Fuller. Miss Smith married Dr. Fayette Clappe, and in 1849 they went around the Horn to San Francisco, where he practiced medicine, then, for reasons of health, moved to the dryer climate of mining country. They were divorced in 1857. The 23 Shirley letters, written by Mrs. Clappe to her sister, Mary-Jane Smith, tell in graphic detail, enlivened by humor and irony, of life at Rich Bar and Indian Bar in 1851-52. The letters were published in the *Pioneer,* a monthly founded in San Francisco in 1854. For modern editions, see Bibliography. Shirley quotations in this text are from the 1949 edition.

10 Uncle Zenas / Cadez Orion, *Miners' Decree; or, a New Verse-ion of the Ten Commandments.* Lettersheet, n.d.

10 "to distant, dangerous starvation points" / Auburn *Placer Herald,* April 3, 1869.

11 "Why this haste" / San Francisco *Hesperian,* I No. 6 (July 15, 1858), 88. "Why neglect the improvement of your mind," she scolded, "the cultivation of your heart, deprive yourself of social intercourse, shut yourself out from society and human sympathy—why?"

11 "The miners of the Sacramento basin" / *Alta,* April 23, 1863.

11 "In a few weeks / Santa Clara *Union* n.d., reprinted in *National,* January 23, 1869.

12 outcroppings / The part of an ore-bearing vein that appears above the surface is called the cropping or outcrop.

12 Humboldt district / For the story of Mark Twain's journey to the Humboldt district and his experiences there, see *Roughing It,* chaps. XXVI-XXIX.

13 "adventurers who failed to find" / *Press,* XIII, No. 14 (October 6, 1866), 211.

13 "the good things" / "Hidden Treasure," *Transcript,* March 31, 1882.

13 "When I left old New York" / "Hunting After Gold," *Put's Original California Songster* (San Francisco, 1868), 23. In wide cir-

culation were many pocket-sized song books of melodies sung in mining camps and theaters: *California Songster* (San Francisco, 1855); *Bella Union Melodeon Songster* (San Francisco, 1860); *The Sally Come up Songster* (San Francisco, 1860); *Champagne Charlie and Coal Oil Tommy Songster* (San Francisco, 1868); *Josh Davis' My Wife's Mother's Gone Home Songster* (San Francisco, n.d.); and numerous others.

13 "run on golden beds" / Lettersheet, *Miner's Life—Illustrated* (Sacramento, c. 1850).

13 "He who comes to the mines" / "Poor Diggings," *Gold Digger's Song Book* (Marysville, 1856), 9.

13 "I saw in dreams" / Alonzo Delano, *The Miner's Progress* (Sacramento, 1853), 6.

13 "I've picked and dug" / "Miner's Lament," *California Songster* (San Francisco, 1855).

13 "With woolen shirt" / "The Happy Miner," *Put's Golden Songster* (San Francisco, n.d.), 44.

13 "For five score" / "Lamentations of a Gold Digger," San Andreas *Independent,* May 9, 1857.

15 Jackass Hill and Angel's Camp / See Mark Twain's Notebook #3 (1865), The Mark Twain Papers, University of California, Berkeley.

15 "But when they talk of cooking" / "The Happy Miner."

15 Alonzo Delano (1806–74). He was an Argonaut whose overland journey was beset with cholera, food shortage and skirmishes with Indians. He began writing in San Francisco, where he had a produce business until cleaned out by fire. Familiar with mining country and a favorite of miners, he adopted the nom de plume of Old Block and exploited traditional California humor in many reminiscences of mining life. See Bibliography.

16 "I never changed" / "The Happy Miner."

16 Piety Hill / This camp was a part of Nevada City south of Deer Creek. Two roads leading to it were called Jacob's Ladder and Tribulation Trail. The ladies of the camp changed the name to Willand Place.

16 "most affectionately and confidentially" / J. D. Borthwick, *Three Years in California,* 193.

16 "Drunk, drunk" / Letter from Henry Jacob on "Society in the Mines," North San Juan *Hydraulic Press,* October 30, 1858. The bottle was a great source of inspiration, courage and comfort. If a teetotal mining camp ever existed in California, historians

have overlooked it. Saloons were numerous and well publicized. An ad in the *Gazette,* May 14, 1864, said: "One Hundred Thousand Square Drinkers Wanted at Blaze's." Another in the same paper, September 14, 1866, promised: "25,000 drinks and 100 Gallons No. one Lager Beer (more or less) for sale daily at John Hahn's Nevada Saloon." In 1853 the *Journal* reported that San Francisco had 537 liquor dispensaries and 743 bartenders of both sexes. The GV *Union,* April 21, 1867, gave Denver barroom rules, two of which were: "Any one refusing to drink when asked will be ignominiously kicked out. No gentlemen are expected to eat the lemon peel in their cocktails, and those who do will not be supplied with any more, and will not be considered gentlemen in future."

17 "I thought it was" / Mariposa *Gazette,* November 1, 1859.

17 "the vice" / Grass Valley *Telegraph,* October 13, 1853. The editor sternly reprimanded the rowdies: "In the gambling and drinking saloons may be seen those on whose cheek would once have mantled the burning blush of shame at the bare suspicion that *they* would ever thus demean themselves."

17 "the most peaceable" / Letter from Veritan, *Journal,* May 9, 1855.

19 Lecture lyceums / The North San Juan *Hydraulic Press* said, February 5, 1859: "The Campo Seco Lyceum was lately honored by having a lady, Mrs. Maria Hill, read before it an original essay on 'Woman's Virtues and Her Errors.'"

19 fiction titles / A few other titles are: "The Dark Morning and the Golden Day," "Howard, the Orphan Apprentice," "The Solitary Grave," "Ben Bolt and Sweet Alice," "Blanche Blakeley; or, the Curse of Beauty." Not all fiction was mawkish, but there was enough of it to induce a vogue of condensed novels that satirized the moony and melodramatic. Bret Harte wrote a number of them, Prentice Mulford and others. Even Mark Twain tried his hand a time or two.

20 " 'Twas evening's hour" / J. W. W., "Mount Shasta, at Sunset," Yreka *Weekly Union,* July 24, 1859.

20 "hie to some sequestered spot" / M., "Adieu to California," San Andreas *Independent,* July 25, 1857. Another example, "Reveries," *Journal,* September 12, 1856, begins: "August, the youngest child of summer, has left us, and September, the firstling of Autumn, drops a tear to her memory."

20 Little Nell / Francis Jeffrey, Scottish Lord-advocate and stern

editor of the *Edinburgh Review,* was moved to tears by the death of Little Nell. Probably miners, tough though they might be, were also affected by fictional pathos and bathos. At any rate, they read a good deal of that sort of thing and apparently enjoyed it. Among *Golden Era* writers were some, like Fanny Fern, Kate Cowslip, Elsie Elfin and Amandy Minnie Douglas, who exemplified the soft period in our literature that has been called the Feminine Fifties. Male authors did not always avoid the saccharine either. James Pipes of Pipesville (Stephen G. Massett) could be maudlin enough to out-Dickens Dickens. The miners of Bret Harte's story, "The Luck of Roaring Camp," seem at first glance to be too stagy and sentimental, but perhaps they should be looked at more closely.

20 "With what emphasis" / "Mining Scenes and Sketches by an Old Miner," San Francisco *Wide West,* August 13, 1854. See also: "An Evening in the Mines," San Andreas *Independent,* September 24, 1856; "Extracts from a Lecture by an old Prospector," *Transcript,* July 29, 1882.

21 "When all the girls" / *Miner's Life—Illustrated.*

21 "The Five H's" / *Era,* XII, No. 12 (February 21, 1864). The contributor of the "Hot whiskey punch" addition was John K. Lovejoy, gusty editor of the Virginia *Old Piute.*

21 "Home!" / Juveniles, "Home, and the Miner," *Journal,* December 23, 1853.

22 "The typical American miner" / "Our Miners Photographed," GV *Union,* May 28, 1871.

23 blind lead / A blind lead is a ledge that does not show on the surface. Mark Twain says in *Roughing It:* "A miner does not know where to look for blind leads, but they are often stumbled upon by accident in the course of driving a tunnel or sinking a shaft."

23 Potosi Company / In 1864 the company gave notice to vacate, but apparently it did not succeed in evicting property owners, who fought back with legal aid.

23 hydraulic mining / The great quantity of debris washed into rivers by this form of mining—46,000,000 cubic yards in 1880 alone—posed such a pressing problem that, as ranchers gained numbers and power, a long and bitter fight ensued between them and hydraulic miners. For years California papers were full of the subject, editors and correspondents violently partisan, litigation widespread. The climax came in 1884, when the state Su-

preme Court issued a permanent injunction against hydraulic mining on the watershed of the Sacramento and San Joaquin Rivers. Although the Caminetti Act, passed by Congress in 1893, provided for control of debris by the use of wing dams, hydraulic mining did not regain its former importance. See: *Report of the Hydraulic Mining Commission,* etc.; also Charles Howard Shinn, *Mining Camps.*

23 "the ruthless power" / *Gazette,* n.d., reprinted in Watsonville, *Pajaro Valley Times,* May 5, 1866.

23 "The 'Big Thing'" *News,* March 22, 1864.

24 "In the hollows" / Charles Howard Shinn, *Mining Camps,* 145.

## 2. Excelsior

26 "Poore leane hungry" / VC *Union,* September 2, 1865.

26 "huge old, rough mass" / *Ibid.,* August 22, 1865.

27 "the most beautiful lake" / *Ibid.,* July 29, 1865.

27 gold-bearing ledges / A ledge is a fissure, filled with mineral, in the country rock. The terms "ledge," "lode," and "vein" are used indiscriminately.

28 "so that the sports" / VC *Union,* August 22, 1865.

29 Hartley / The biographical data here come chiefly from a Pioneer Record filed in the California State Library, Sacramento, by Hartley's grand niece, Mrs. Claudia Wheat. There are various other stories about him. A common remark is that he had been proprietor of a bookstore in Philadelphia. Perhaps. Another is that he went West in search of health, but he certainly seemed robust enough as trapper and miner at Meadow Lake. One account says that soon after taking to the woods he teamed up with a man known as Tennessee Targus or Carriger, that they worked trap lines together and prospected together. Some historians say that Hartley's Dutch Flat relative, Frank Picking, was also associated with them in mining. At this late date it is difficult to confirm or disprove any of these details. For biographical summaries, see: VC *Union,* December 20, 1865; *Sun,* June 9, 1866; GV *Union,* August 19, 1963; Thompson and West, *History of Nevada County* (1880).

29 windward side / See "The Hermit of Meadow Lake," San Francisco *Examiner,* n.d., reprinted in *Republican,* October 26, 1887.

30 "would saw on" / Clarence M. Wooster, "Railroading in California in the Seventies," 366.

## 3. Gold Rush 1865

33 "specimens shown to us" / GV *Union,* June 27, 1865.

33 "This new mining district" / *Stars and Stripes,* July 12, 1865.

33 20-stamp mill / Stamps were the ore-crushing agents used in the conventional method of milling gold-bearing quartz. Set up usually in batteries of five, average weight about 800 pounds, they crushed the rock in a wet process that allowed the gold to amalgamate with mercury. The mercury was then recovered by retorting, or distillation, and the gold was cast into a bar or brick. For an exposition of milling techniques in general use at that time, see: *The Miner's Own Book;* E. M. and M. L. Wade, *Compendium of Gold Metallurgy.*

33 "being actively worked" / VC *Union,* June 23, 1865.

34 "The town site" / Letter from Alpha, *Appeal,* July 30, 1865.

34 "but when the dark object" / Letter from Excelsior, June 25, 1865, *Enquirer,* July 1, 1865.

35 speculators / The writer of the above letter remarked: "I believe that every branch of business has found a speculator. The only thing left will be to build a church."

35 "One 'horn'" / In western bar language, a horn was a drink, quantity not clearly defined. In Virginia City the standard tot of whiskey or brandy was 2½ ounces. Possibly Meadow Lake barkeeps followed suit.

36 "the prettiest site" / *Messenger,* August 5, 1865.

37 "Commencing at Culbert's Bridge" / GV *Union,* July 18, 1865.

38 "The dust is deep" / "California Stage Company," *Put's Golden Songster,* 31.

38 horn / Short for hornspoon: a longitudinal section cut from the under side of an ox horn and scraped thin. It was used for washing gold-bearing gravel and pulp where delicate tests were required. An experienced miner usually carried a horn.

38 "a very tall" / Letter from Alf Doten, August 14, 1865, VC *Union,* August 17, 1865.

39 hurdy-gurdy / A flutelike stringed instrument, the sound produced by the friction of a resined wheel turned by a crank. The name was a standard label for a dance hall, no matter what sort of music was provided. Hurdy-gurdy was also a term used in mining for a water wheel propelled by the impact of a stream of water upon its paddles.

39 "the voluptuous feminine" / Dayton, Nevada, *Lyon County Sentinel,* March 7, 1866.

40 "boiled and surged" / Letter from Scruggs, Jr., July 24, 1865, *Messenger,* July 29, 1865.

40 "Seventy-five houses" / Marysville *Appeal,* August 20, 1865.

41 ten long letters / Doten's Meadow Lake letters were published in the VC *Union,* August 11, 13 (two letters), 15, 17, 19, 22 (two letters), 23, 1865. One letter was lost in the mail.

41 "We had the first shave" / *Republican,* April 18, 1883.

42 "We climbed" / VC *Union,* August 15, 1865.

42 "cannot be mistaken" / *Ibid.,* September 17, 1865.

44 "I am confident" / Traveler, "Visit to Excelsior District," Marysville *Appeal,* October 22, 1865. This correspondent said that, having been given feet in Excelsior mines called Scalped Emigrant, Tight Rope and Sure to Find It, he started out to visit the district but did not get there. "I never was at Summit City," he said, "never intend to go there . . . and I don't believe there is such a place. . . ."

44 "The vein rock" / Dogberry (Prentice Mulford), "Geology and Geologists," San Francisco *Golden Era,* December 31, 1865.

44 hanging wall / The wall or side over the vein.

44 foot wall / The upper surface of the rock that lies under the lode or vein; also called the lower or underlying wall.

44 country rock / The rock traversed by or adjacent to a lode or ore deposit.

44 "Know all men" / *Stars and Stripes,* December 31, 1868.

44 "There is undoubtedly" / New York *Graphic,* April 7, 1880.

45 mining laws / Nevada County mining laws required that twenty days of labor or $100 be annually expended on a claim. If the owner failed to comply, his claim could be relocated.

46 "this noted district" / VC *Union,* August 23, 1865.

46 "We do not hesitate" / *Enquirer,* n.d., reprinted in *Gazette,* July 19, 1865.

46 "croppings from" / VC *Union,* July 21, 1865.

46 "I have seen it all" / Letter from T. H., August 8, 1865, *Appeal,* August 11, 1865.

46 wildcat / A wildcat claim was undeveloped or unproved mining ground, hence of conjectural or doubtful value. In Washoe, any claim not on the main Comstock lode was called wildcat. In a mining district there was generally a good deal of speculation in wildcat stocks.

46 "All day the noise" / VC *Union,* August 13, 1865.

46 "By Shesuskrist" / *Ibid.*

47 "the people" / Letter from Brick, September 21, 1865, VC *Union,* September 24, 1865.

47 "there is brought" / Letter from M. H. Crandall, Washoe City, Nevada, *Times,* n.d., reprinted in *Gazette,* September 11, 1865.

48 "The open lot" / Letter from L., *Press,* XI, No. 12 (September 23, 1865), 179.

49 "filled with a population" / Letter from B., February 7, 1866, VC *Union,* February 9, 1866.

49 rocker / Also called a cradle, it was a short trough fitted with hopper, apron and riffles for washing gold-bearing gravel. In Old Block's *The Miner's Progress,* the Pilgrim, laboring in the diggings, says: "So, here condemned by Fates unkind, / I rock illusive sand, / And dream of wailing babes at home, / Unrocked, an orphan band."

51 "positively required" / *News,* June 13, 1866.

52 "There is a chance" / VC *Union,* August 23, 1865.

52 "bring to my mind" / Letter from Pip, August 23, 1865, *News,* August 25, 1865.

52 "Society in this place" / VC *Union,* August 15, 1865.

53 "by aid of burnt cork" / *News,* September 22, 1865.

53 "The genial countenance" / VC *Union,* August 19, 1865.

53 "to our utter astonishment" / Letter from T. H., September 19, 1865, *Appeal,* September 23, 1865.

54 "Hello, Bob!" / "A Meadow Lake Hotel," *Enterprise,* n.d., reprinted in GV *Union,* August 12, 1877.

55 "We have seen" / VC *Union,* October 1, 1865.

## 4. Sierra Winter 1865–66

56 "on the very summit" / *Messenger,* n.d., reprinted in *Stars and Stripes,* February 8, 1866.

57 "our snow shoe heeled" / Letter from Pine Martin, January 23, 1866, VC *Union,* January 29, 1866.

57 "What Peter, the Hermit" / Letter from B., February 7, 1866, VC *Union,* February 9, 1866.

58 "have become experts" / *Messenger,* n.d., reprinted in *Stars and Stripes,* February 7, 1866.

58 "a prepossessing damsel" / "Snowshoeing at Meadow Lake," *Enquirer,* April 14, 1866.

60 "calls upon" / *News,* December 1, 1865.

60 "would think he was" / VC *Union,* February 9, 1866.

61 "the learned ex-public" / Letter from B., April 20, 1866, VC *Union,* April 23, 1866. Orion Clemens had also served as Acting Governor of Nevada Territory. About his learning, he was an idealist who delved into the lore of political ideas and a variety of religions, frequently changing his allegiance to church and party. In Mark Twain's narrative, "Indiantown" (c. 1899), the character of George Harrison seems modeled after Orion Clemens: e.g., "He had been a Presbyterian, a Baptist, a Methodist, an Episcopalian, an infidel, a Mohammedan; had been three times forward and back over the course and was now a Presbyterian again and due to rebecome a Baptist in thirteen months."

61 "we have a meeting" / Letter from Comanche, January 9, 1866, VC *Union,* January 13, 1866.

62 "the usual number" / Letter from B., February 7, 1866, VC *Union,* February 9, 1866.

62 "one of the sovereigns" / *Ibid.*

62 "watched from the rising" / *News,* January 22, 1866.

63 cleanup / The operation of collecting the gold or silver taken out during a single run of a stamp mill, hydraulic, or drift claim.

63 "took this doubting Thomas" / *Press,* XII, No. 5 (February 3, 1866), 73.

64 "Mountain towns" / *Enquirer,* n.d., reprinted in *Gazette,* March 13, 1866.

65 "I can compare" / Letter from B., March 4, 1866, VC *Union,* March 6, 1866.

66 "will be 10,000" / Letter from Summit City, February 12, 1866, *Messenger*, February 24, 1866.

66 "will rise" / Sacramento *Union,* n.d., reprinted in *Transcript,* May 13, 1866.

### 5. Stampede to Meadow Lake 1866

67 " 'thick as autumn leaves' " / Letter from B., April 20, 1866, VC *Union,* April 23, 1866.

67 "The only sensation" / Letter from Quitman, May 17, 1866, *Enquirer,* May 19, 1866.

68 "I would advise" / Letter from Brier, *News,* March 28, 1866.

69 "It is almost impossible" / Noiro (Orion Clemens), "Our Ledges

—No. 8," *Sun,* July 2, 1866. "I have not counted the number of carpenters," he said, "but I suppose, at a rough guess, there are about a thousand, each working with both hands at once, a hammer in one hand and a saw in the other."

70 potatoes, flour, bacon / Potatoes sold at 10¢ a pound, bacon 40¢, beef 16¢, coffee 50¢, tea $1.25, flour $7 a hundred-weight, molasses $2 a gallon. These prices were high for the times.

70 "Hair 7" / Traveler, "Visit to Excelsior District," Marysville *Appeal,* October 22, 1865.

70 "Snow, 'feet' " / Letter from Quitman, May 17, 1866, *Enquirer,* May 19, 1866.

70 "quite a gay little craft" / Letter from A. D. G. Mead, June 8, 1866, Colusa *Sun,* June 23, 1866.

70 bit-house / As the name implied, a bit-house purveyed cheap drinks, generally diluted. Watering down was a trick of the trade. "A Reminiscence," San Andreas *Independent,* January 10, 1857, tells of three merchandisers of '49 who started for the mines with nine pack mules loaded with goods: "The cargo consisted of eight five-gallon kegs of brandy; two cases of absynthe; seven cases of brandy; some *bad* whisky; eight dozen clay pipes; three dozen shirts, and a lot of blankets and *etceteras;* valued as follows: . . . absynthe, $20.00 per bottle; brandy the same; that in the kegs we retailed at one ounce the tin-cupfull, or $2.00 the drink, (and as we had so many running streams to cross, it stretched out amazingly;) . . ."

71 "elevated her lower limb" / Letter from B., May 5, 1866, VC *Union,* May 8, 1866.

71 new towns / It may be observed in passing that the names of these towns were more dignified, more solemn, than the slap-dash, ironical, sometimes ribald, names of early mining camps. See note on place names, 177.

71 "bid fair to become" / *Sun,* June 18, 1866.

72 "forcibly reminded" / Letter from O. I. S., May 15, 1866, VC *Union,* May 17, 1866.

73 "cursed with a mining" / *Messenger,* August 11, 1866.

76 "after which the would-be" / *Sun,* June 15, 1866.

76 "Arrivals from" / Letter from A. D. G. Mead, June 18, 1866, Colusa *Sun,* June 23, 1866.

76 "Distinguished arrivals" / VC *Union,* May 25, 1866.

77 "all kinds of refreshments" / *Sun,* June 6, 1866.

78 "We might walk" / *Ibid.,* June 15, 1866.

78 "is a very poor place" / *News,* June 27, 1866.

79 "We know of several" / Washoe City, Nevada, *Eastern Slope,* August 4, 1866.

79 "The majority" / Letter from Typo, June 20, 1866, San Rafael *Marin County Journal,* July 14, 1866.

79 "One year ago" / *Sun,* n.d. reprinted in News, July 20, 1866.

80 "Before another year" / *Transcript,* June 2, 1866.

80 "Near a calm Lake" / "Excelsior," by Waif, *Sun,* June 9, 1866.

80 "Excelsior!" / M. Y. D., "The Storm Spirit of Excelsior," *Ibid.,* June 27, 1866.

80 "New Exhibition" / *Ibid.,* June 30, 1866.

80 "under the able direction" / *Ibid.,* June 27, 1866.

## 6. Sierra Summer 1866

82 "All the hillsides" / *Sun,* July 21, 1866.

83 "Dan is now engaged" / VC *Union,* July 28, 1866.

83 "Everybody that can get away" / Letter from Uncle John, August 2, 1866, Downieville *Sierra Advocate,* August 11, 1866.

84 "we see men" / GV *Union,* August 11, 1866.

84 "the biggest bilk" / *Appeal,* August 11, 1866.

84 "At Huffaker's" / *Transcript,* March 6, 1888. The paper said that the author, Judge Goodwin, "now of the Salt Lake Tribune, was one of the first to be seized with the fever and . . . one of the first to recover."

85 "The *bourse* was flat" / Letter from W., *Transcript,* August 12, 1866.

85 "will be set apart" / *Sun,* August 13, 1866.

86 "We cannot but notice" / *Ibid.*

87 "Let those who are" / *Transcript,* September 9, 1866.

87 "Pealed noses" / *Sun,* October 8, 1866.

88 "After the lacing up" / VC *Union,* October 4, 1866.

88 chlorination process / For an exposition of this process, see: G. F. Deetken, "Meadow Lake and the Chlorination Process." Since the story of the Meadow Lake region is not intended to be a technological treatise, details of Deetken's process and of other processes mentioned later have been omitted from the text.

88 "In every fever" / Letter from J .S. L., September 22, 1866, *Press,* XIII, No. 14 (October 6, 1866), 211. The writer admitted that the town "is in so low a condition at present, that her death has been already reported by her enemies, and daily looked for, with trembling, by some of her too credulous friends."

89 "We have built" / *Sun,* n.d., reprinted in *Press,* XIII, No. 15 (October 13, 1866), 230.

89 "Miss Pittsinger" / *Sun,* October 8, 1866.

90 *Bugle Peals* / Said the *Sun,* October 18, 1866: "Miss P. may be called the Poetess of the American War—the strife . . . awakened . . . the noblest faculties . . . of the lady, and developed a genius of which, possibly, not even the possessor was conscious."

90 "has gained" / *Transcript,* November 29, 1866.

90 "Enchanting region!" / *Sun,* February 2, 1867.

91 Mark Twain / Having heard of the rush to Meadow Lake, he was sufficiently interested to go out of his way to visit the place, which gave him, as a newspaper correspondent, a subject to write about. His brother, Orion, had left town about three months before. Mark Twain's comments, subtitled "A Memento of Speculation," are from his "Interior Notes—No. 2," *Bulletin,* December 6, 1866.

91 "I verily believe" / Letter from Seymour Pixley, September 30, 1866, *News,* October 12, 1866.

92 "It is expected" / GV *Union,* December 13, 1866.

## 7. Uncertain Year 1866–67

94 "Where is Meadow Lake?" / *News,* March 26, 1867.

95 "This House and Lot" / Letter from S. X., March 24, 1867, *Transcript,* March 28, 1867.

95 "Nothing on a bright" / *Transcript,* December 7, 1866.

95 "Talk about a divine" / Eureka *Sentinel,* n.d., reprinted in *Transcript,* May 22, 1875.

96 "as sweet a little" / Letter from S. X., *Transcript,* March 19, 1867.

96 "the beauty and chivalry" / *Ibid.*

96 "that the Marshals" / *Sun,* January 5, 1867.

96 "It may surprise" / Letter from S. X., March 24, 1867, *Transcript,* March 28, 1867.

97 "No sun, no moon" / *Sun,* January 26, 1867. The lines were lifted, in part, from a short poem by Thomas Hood, about the somberness of November and entitled merely "No!" The editor of the *Sun* did not identify the author, perhaps thinking that for informed readers there was no need to do so.

97 "Meadow Lake!" *Ibid.,* February 2, 1867.

98 "Nowhere, within the range" / *Ibid.,* March 2, 1867.

98 "there is no doubt" / *Ibid.,* January 19, 1867.

98 "one of the richest" / *Transcript,* December 9, 1866.

98 "a quantity of" / *Enterprise,* April 7, 1867.

99 "All agree" / "Our Prospects," *Sun,* April 13, 1867.

99 "We now hope" / Letter from S. X., March 15, 1867, *Transcript,* March 19, 1867.

100 "sane men" / *Gazette,* June 13, 1867.

101 "It is unusual" / *Sun,* August 1, 1867.

102 shotgun messenger / This important functionary, with shotgun at the ready, rode the company's Concord coaches to protect bullion shipments from highwaymen. The company generously rewarded messengers and drivers who shot it out with road agents. When Venard killed three bandits who held up the North San Juan stage, he was given $3,000 and a Henry rifle, on the stock of which was a silver plate that depicted the exploit and bore the inscription: "Presented by Wells Fargo & Co. to Stephen Venard for his gallant conduct May 16, 1866."

102 "the fire out" / *Sun,* October 5, 1867.

102 "His wife" / "Poor Old Meadow Lake," *Enterprise,* n.d., reprinted in *Sun,* August 24, 1867.

102 "one of the class" / *Sun,* August 24, 1867.

103 open ledges in depth / The deepest Meadow Lake shaft was that of the Excelsior mine, which eventually reached 185 feet. Otherwise, few got down as far as fifty feet. The shallowness led mining experts at the time, and especially many years later, to speculate on possible results had Meadow Lake shafts penetrated further. Perhaps mining authorities were influenced by the great profits of the Comstock Big Bonanza, when shafts of the best-known companies went down 1,900 to 3,500 feet. At Meadow Lake, the disappointing truth was that nearly all the richness was on the surface or not far below it.

103 "will be the means" / *Sun,* July 20, 1867.

103 "are very flattering" / *Enterprise,* July 31, 1867.

103 "the Spring-time" / *Sun,* September 10, 1867.

104 "some have already" / Grass Valley *National,* December 9, 1867.

8. Long Road Down 1867–74

105 "The Meadow Lake denizens" / Auburn *Placer Herald,* April 4, 1868.

106 "two restaurants" / Letter from Snow Ball, July 23, 1868, *En-*

*quirer,* July 25, 1868. Despite the unpromising condition of the town, Snow Ball affirmed that "this is now the richest mining District in the State of California—let those who doubt it come and satisfy themselves."

106 "This place at present" / *Enterprise,* July 21, 1868.

106 "The prospects" / *Transcript,* July 8, 1868.

107 "The many stockholders" / *Enterprise,* October 20, 1868.

108 "The last assessment" / *Transcript,* October 11, 1868.

108 tailings / Debris left after milling, also the detritus discharged from hydraulic mines. In California, hydraulic debris was generally called "slickens," and the quantity was tremendous. (See note on hydraulic mining, 156.) Some gold was always lost in tailings, which were often reworked. On the Mother Lode, Chinese miners, who followed in the wake of white miners, made a living out of this debris. Sam Clemens, after failing to strike it rich in Esmeralda in 1862, got a job screening tailings in a quartz mill. See *Roughing It,* chap. XXXVI.

108 "It is probable" / *Transcript,* September 11, 1868.

108 "The mines are said" / *Tribune,* November 7, 1868.

109 "is now about to shuffle" / GV *Union,* December 23, 1868.

109 "houses with all" / Edwin Franklin Morse, "The Story of a Gold Miner," 344.

110 Burns process / For a description of the Burns process, see: *Transcript,* August 18, 1869; *Enterprise,* August 25, 1868; October 8, 1869.

110 "People who have examined" / *Gazette,* June 17, 1869.

110 "Meadow Lake will soon" / *Transcript,* July 20, 1869.

110 "Since the success" / *Ibid.,* August 18, 1869.

110 "and all able to work" / *Messenger,* October 16, 1869.

111 "If it does not pay" / *Transcript,* September 2, 1869.

111 Churchill process / For a description of this process, see: *Enterprise,* October 8, 1869; *Messenger,* October 18, 1869.

111 Hartley process / Hartley kept his process a secret, but was said to have deposited the formula in the safe of Booth & Co., Sacramento, and to have arranged that, in event of his death, the process be given to Franklin Cook and John Clark. See letter from Clark, Transcript, n.d., reprinted in *Press,* LXVI, No. 5 (February 4, 1893), 69.

111 "After four years' time" / *Messenger,* November 6, 1869.

111 "those who have been" / *Transcript,* June 19, 1870.

112 "still are firm" / *Enterprise,* January 21, 1870.

113 "The mining prospects" / *Transcript,* September 4, 1870.

114 "Of all the eloquent" / Stephen Powers, "A City of a Day," 430, 438.

115 "that the sight" / *Bulletin,* n.d., reprinted in *Transcript,* June 13, 1873.

115 "feels quite confident" / *Bulletin,* n.d., reprinted in *Republican,* June 12, 1873.

115 "But, with all its" / *Enterprise,* September 12, 1873.

115 "that a better day" / *Press,* n.d., reprinted in Jackson *Amador Dispatch,* July 5, 1873.

116 "Thus Meadow Lake" / Letter from Meadow Lake, September 27, 1873, San Francisco *Chronicle,* October 2, 1873.

## 9. Indian Summer 1875–80

117 "Virginia City contributed" / "Another Mining Revival," *Enterprise,* May 24, 1875.

117 "would please" / *Transcript,* October 4, 1873.

118 "It may be" / GV *Union,* February 5, 1875.

119 "There seems to be" / *Republican,* April 28, 1875.

120 Fryer process / For a description of this process, see: *100 Years of Nevada County,* 63; GV *Union,* April 4, 1876.

120 "Mr. Fryer" / *Transcript,* January 4, 1876.

121 "gold by the ton" / *Enterprise,* n.d., reprinted in GV *Union,* June 12, 1875.

121 "will very shortly" / GV *Union,* June 22, 1875.

121 "assures us" / *Tidings,* July 17, 1875.

121 "The miners of the coast" / New York *Herald,* December 28, 1875.

121 "Comstock bonanzas" / There were flush times on the Comstock in 1862–64, but they were eclipsed by the boom of the 1870's. In those years the Big Bonanza, as it was called, took out about $300,000,000 in silver, brought prosperity to many, and made fortunes for the four Bonanza Kings: John W. Mackay, James G. Fair, William S. O'Brien, and James C. Flood.

121 "We obtained the impression" / *Enterprise,* August 7, 1875.

123 "Both of them" / North San Juan *Times,* December 25, 1875.

123 "Everybody that pretends" / *Republican,* November 10, 1875.

123 "these carping critics" / *Transcript,* March 10, 1876.

123 "when all my esteemed" / Letter from Robert M. Fryer, November 9, 1875, GV *Union,* November 19, 1875.

124 Independence Day / For the story of the Independence Day demonstration of the Fryer process, see: *100 Years of Nevada County,* 63. Contemporary newspapers do not mention this occasion, nor does any other Meadow Lake historian.

124 "the richness of the rock" / Letter from Robert M. Fryer, September 5, 1879, "The Fryer Process," GV *Union,* September 7, 1879.

125 "they feel confident" / *Enterprise,* n.d., reprinted in *Transcript,* September 17, 1876.

125 "represents things" / *Ibid.*

125 "We hate to think it" / GV *Union,* August 3, 1877.

125 Schiveley brothers / For details of the Schiveley process, see: *Republican,* September 4, 1878: *Forum,* September 12, 1878.

126 Willard process / For a description of this process, see: GV *Union,* September 1, 1878.

126 "Gold!" *Republican,* August 17, 1878.

126 "With the certainty" / *Ibid.,* August 28, 1878.

126 "a grand rush" / *Ibid.*

126 "discloses richer" / *Ibid.,* November 16, 1878.

126 "it is estimated" / *Ibid.*

127 Gould process / For a description of this process, see: GV *Union,* September 4, 1879; *Tidings,* September 6, 1879; *Press,* XL, No. 5 (January 31, 1880), 73; *Republican,* September 8, 1880.

127 "At Last!" *Republican,* September 6, 1879.

127 "Meadow Lake will yet" / GV *Union,* November 2, 1879.

127 "we doubt not" / Letter from J. J. Owens to San Jose *Mercury,* n.d., reprinted in *Republican,* January 3, 1880.

128 "Those who have held" / *Republican,* May 29, 1880.

128 "just as enthusiastic" / *Ibid.,* November 3, 1880.

128 bonded four mines / To bond a mine is to take an option on it by making a down payment. Hartley's $8,000 would be paid, not in a lump sum, but piecemeal in the manner of instalment buying of today.

128 "swarm of so-called" / New York *Daily Graphic,* April 16, 1880.

129 "ten men" / Virginia *Chronicle,* n.d., reprinted in GV *Union,* July 30, 1879.

129 "The Haunted House" / A long poem in three parts. Part I, which describes "An old deserted Mansion" and its uncared-for surroundings, is also descriptive of the dying town of Meadow Lake. For example, stanza six: "No human figure stirr'd, to go or come, / No face look'd forth from shut or open casement;

/ No chimney smoked—there was no sign of Home / From parapet to basement."

## 10. Hope Deferred 1881–92

131 "which have been lingering" / "Old Meadow Lake," *Press,* XLIII, No. 11 (September 10, 1881), 174.

131 "The predictions" / *Republican,* n.d., reprinted in *Press,* XLIII, No. 11 (September 10, 1881), 174.

132 "They say" *Republican,* June 17, 1882.

132 "In the course of time" / *Enterprise,* n.d., reprinted in *Transcript,* April 23, 1882.

133 opulent gold regions / For thirty years or more, the mines around Nevada City and Grass Valley had been producing yearly, on the average, some two to three million in gold bullion.

133 "When you have given / *Transcript,* n.d., reprinted in *Republican,* September 13, 1883.

133 "We are" / *Tidings,* September 18, 1886.

133 "by practical experience" / *Republican,* August 20, 1884.

133 "Last week" / Reno, Nevada, *Gazette,* n.d., reprinted in *Republican,* October 6, 1886.

134 "it is confidently" / Virginia *Chronicle,* n.d., reprinted in *Republican,* September 11, 1886.

134 "It is predicted" / *Republican,* September 11, 1886.

134 "As to the coming" / Reno, Nevada, *Gazette,* n.d., reprinted in *Tidings,* October 16, 1886.

134 "It seems hard" / Virginia *Chronicle,* n.d., reprinted in *Republican,* September 11, 1886.

134 "He says" / Sierra City *Tribune,* n.d., reprinted in *Republican,* August 3, 1887.

135 "There is no doubt" / *Republican,* n.d., reprinted in GV *Union,* November 1, 1887.

136 Morris process / For an explanation of this process, see: *Tidings,* November 30, 1888; "Meadow Lake District," *Eighth Annual Report of the State Mineralogist,* 364.

136 "There is a probability" / *Tidings,* August 3, 1888.

137 "there is an abundance" / *Republican,* n.d., reprinted in *Press,* LIII, No. 7 (August 14, 1886), 97.

137 "comparatively deserted" / *Enterprise,* n.d., reprinted in *Transcript,* September 12, 1889.

138 "a number of practical" / Sierra City *Tribune,* n.d., reprinted in *Transcript,* June 24, 1890.

138 "There will unquestionably" / Letter from R. C. G., *Press,* LXI, No. 25 (December 20, 1890), 394.

138 "It is understood" / *Republican,* n.d., reprinted in *Tidings,* November 6, 1891.

## 11. Aftermath 1893–

142 shooting and trial / For accounts of these events, see: San Francisco *Call,* July 27, 28, September 14, 1894; San Francisco *Examiner,* July 27, 28, 1894; Virginia *Chronicle,* July 27, August 4, September 11, 13, 17, 1894; January 12, 1895.

143 "The most disastrous" / Dan De Quille, "A Brief Golden Dream," 150.

143 "Considering the difficulties" / Waldemar Lindgren, "The Auriferous Veins of the Meadow Lake District, California," 206.

143 "Some day" / Dan De Quille, "A Brief Golden Dream," 150.

143 "It is reported" / "Meadow Lake Again," *Press,* LXX, No. 4 (January 26, 1895), 55.

144 Cardwell process / For a description of this process, see: "Mining Summary," *Mining and Scientific Journal,* LXXIV, No. 19 (May 8, 1897), 390.

144 "Scattered veins" / "Meadow Lake Mining District," *Press,* LXXXV, No. 4 (January 25, 1902), 46.

144 "Already prospectors" / "Mining Summary," *Mining and Scientific Journal,* LXXXIX, No. 13 (September 23, 1899).

145 "well defined and important" / Charles W. Raymond, "Meadow Lake Mining District," 46, 48.

145 Wisker / See "The Gold-Bearing Veins of Meadow Lake District, Nevada County." Wisker pointed out that Lindgren, who made an unfavorable report on the district in 1893, "little dreamed . . . that forty years of progress in the mining industry would develop an Alaska Juneau, making a profit from ore averaging less than $1.00 per ton, and that $7.00 ore would furnish a fair profit margin on a quantity basis even under such transportation and climatic conditions as those of Meadow Lake."

146 "If Meadow Lake measures up" / A. L. Wisker, "Can Modern Metallurgical Methods Revitalize the *Meadow Lake* Area?" 104.

147 "Nowhere in the mountains" / Dan De Quille, "A Brief Golden Dream," 150.

# Bibliography

Aaron, Charles Howard. *Leaching Gold and Silver Ores*. San Francisco, 1881.

*Bean's History and Directory of Nevada County, California*. Compiled by Edwin F. Bean. Nevada, 1867.

Borthwick, J. D. *Three Years in California*. Edinburgh, 1857.

Browne, J. Ross. "Meadow Lake District," *Mineral Resources of the States and Territories West of the Rocky Mountains*, 136–37. U. S. Treasury Department, Washington, 1867.

Clappe, Louise Amelia Knapp Smith. *California in 1851. The Letters of Dame Shirley*. San Francisco, 1933.

——. *The Shirley Letters from the California Mines 1851–1852*. Ed. Carl I. Wheat. New York, 1949.

Cummins, Ella Sterling. *The Story of the Files*. San Francisco, 1893.

Deetken, G. F. "Meadow Lake and the Chlorination Process," *Engineering and Mining Journal*, LV, No. 11 (March 18, 1893), 244.

De Groot, Henry. *Recollections of California Mining Life*. San Francisco, 1884.

Delano, Alonzo. *The Idle and the Industrious Miner*. Sacramento, 1854.

——. *The Miner's Progress; or, Scenes in the Life of a California Miner*. Sacramento, 1853.

——. *Old Block's Sketch-Book; or, Tales of California Life*. Sacramento, 1856.

——. *Pen Knife Sketches; or, Chips of the Old Block*. Sacramento, 1853.

De Quille, Dan. "A Brief Golden Dream," *Engineering and Mining Journal*, LV, No. 7 (February 18, 1893), 150.

Eggleston, T. *Leaching Gold and Silver Ores in the West*. n.p., 1883.

"The Elephant as They Saw It." Assembled by Elisabeth L. Egenhoff.

Centennial Supplement to the *California Journal of Mines and Geology* for October, 1949.

"Excelsior," *Mining and Scientific Press,* XII, No. 22 (June 2, 1866), 342.

"Excelsior," *Mining and Scientific Press,* XIV, No. 2 (January 12, 1867), 22.

"Famed Meadow Lake," *Mining and Scientific Press,* LXIX, No. 12 (September 22, 1894), 181.

*Gold Rush Country.* Menlo Park, 1957.

"The Gould Process at Meadow Lake," *Mining and Scientific Press,* XL, No. 5 (January 31, 1880), 73.

"Henness Pass," *P. G. & E. Progress,* XLIV, No. 6 (June, 1967), 8.

*Historical Summary of Gold, Silver, Copper, Lead and Zinc Produced in California, 1848 to 1926.* Bureau of Mines, Washington, 1929.

Hobson, J. B. "Nevada County," *Tenth Annual Report of the State Mineralogist of California.* Sacramento, 1890.

Kinyon, Edmund. *The Northern Mines.* Grass Valley, c. 1949.

"Lager Beer Ledge," *Mining and Scientific Press,* VIII, No. 11 (March 12, 1864), 164.

Lardner, W. B. and M. J. Brock. *History of Placer and Nevada Counties, California.* Los Angeles, 1924.

"A Letter From Meadow Lake," *Nevada County Historical Society,* 5, No. 6 (November, 1951), 3–4.

"Letter from Summit City," *Mining and Scientific Press,* XI, No. 12 (September 23, 1865), 179.

Lindgren, Waldemar. "The Auriferous Veins of the Meadow Lake District, California," *American Journal of Science,* XLVI, (September, 1893), 201–206.

Logan, Clarence A. *Mother Lode Gold Belt of California.* Bulletin No. 108, November, 1934, State of California, Department of Natural Resources, Division of Mines. Sacramento, 1935.

MacBoyle, Errol. "Meadow Lake Mining District," *Mines and Mineral Resources of Nevada County,* 33–37. California State Mining Bureau, San Francisco, December, 1918.

———. *Mines and Mineral Resources of Nevada County.* Sacramento, 1919.

"Meadow Lake," *Mining and Scientific Press,* XL, No. 11 (March 13, 1880), 162.

"Meadow Lake," *Pacific Miner,* X, No. 11 (November, 1906), 28.

"Meadow Lake Again," *Mining and Scientific Press,* LXX, No. 4 (January 26, 1895), 55.

"Meadow Lake District," *Eighth Annual Report of the State Mineralogist.* Sacramento, 1888.

"Meadow Lake District," *Mining and Scientific Press,* XL, No. 25 (June 19, 1880), 386.

"Meadow Lake District," *Mining in California,* California State Mining Bureau, San Francisco, October 1924.

"The Meadow Lake Mines—a Deserted City," *Mining and Scientific Press,* XXVI, No. 25 (June 21, 1873).

*Mineral Commodities of California.* Ed. Lauren A. Wright. State of California, Department of Natural Resources, Division of Mines, San Francisco, December, 1957.

*The Miner's Own Book.* San Francisco, 1858.

*The Miner's Pocket Manual.* San Francisco, c. 1875.

"A Miner's Sunday in Coloma," *Century Magazine,* June, 1891.

*Nevada City Nugget. 100 Years of Nevada County.* Nevada, 1951.

*Nevada County, California. A General and Historical Summary.* Compiled by *Alta California,* Inc. Sacramento, c. 1931.

"The New Excelsior District," *Mining and Scientific Press,* XI, No. 2 (July 15, 1865), 23.

"The New Excelsior District," *Mining and Scientific Press,* XI, No. 13 (September 30, 1865), 199.

"A New Mining District," *Mining and Scientific Press,* X, No. 26 (July 1, 1865), 406.

O'Driscoll, Florence. *Notes on the Treatment of Gold Ores.* New York and London, 1889.

"Old Meadow Lake," *Mining and Scientific Press,* XLIII, No. 11 (September 10, 1881), 174.

Powers, Stephen. "A City of a Day," *Overland Monthly,* 13, No. 5 (November, 1874), 430–38.

Raymond, Charles W. "Meadow Lake Mining District," *Mining and Scientific Press,* LXXXV, No. 4 (January 25, 1902), 46–48.

*Report of the Hydraulic Mining Commission upon the Feasibility of the Resumption of Hydraulic Mining in California. A Report to the Legislature of 1927.* Sacramento, 1927.

Shinn, Charles Howard. *Mining Camps. A Study in American Frontier Government.* New York, 1885.

*South Yuba Water Company.* New York, 1894.

"Summit City—Excelsior Mines," *Mining and Scientific Press,* XI, No. 14 (October 7, 1865), 210.

Wade, E. M. and M. L. *Compendium of Gold Metallurgy.* Los Angeles, 1899.

Walker, Franklin. *San Francisco's Literary Frontier.* New York, 1939.

Whitney, J. D. *The Yosemite Book.* New York, 1868.

Wiltsee, Ernest A. *The Pioneer Miner and the Pack Mule Express.* San Francisco, 1931.

Wisker, A. L. "Can Modern Metallurgical Methods Revitalize the *Meadow Lake* Area?" *Engineering and Mining Journal,* CLV, No. 5 (May, 1958), 104.

——. "The Gold-Bearing Veins of Meadow Lake District, Nevada County," *California Journal of Mines and Geology,* 32, No. 2 (April, 1936), 189–204.

Wooster, Clarence M. "Meadow Lake City and a Winter at Cisco in the Sixties," *California Historical Society Quarterly,* XVIII, No. 2 (June, 1939), 149–56.

——. "Railroading in California in the Seventies," *California Historical Society Quarterly,* XVIII, No. 4 (December, 1939), 355–68.

# Index

175